Overture and Beginners Please

Anthya Cohen

MOVEMENTS

To Joshua, Isaac, Joseph and Louis
To pass on to the sixth generation.

I would like to thank my daughter Gillian
for her imaginative help with the book cover
and for her unwavering encouragement
during the writing of this memoir.

"Remembrance of things past is not necessarily the remembrance of things as they were."

Marcel Proust

"There are some things one remembers even though they may never have happened."

Harold Pinter

PREFACE

Once, many years ago, I decided to write (note: write, not try to write), a Mills and Boon romance. I had the perfect scenario, a young, beautiful, talented girl violinist, and a charismatic young conductor. I knew all about beautiful, young, talented violinists, my daughter being one of them. And I knew about young, charismatic, male conductors, my husband had performed with some. I had it made! I had never read a Mills and Boon book, so I went off to the library and borrowed as many books as possible; hiding them from sight as I was too snobbish to allow anyone to think I read this stuff.

I was amazed to find some very good writing and assumed that it would be a way for a professional writer to earn some extra money; moonlighting, using pseudonyms. I did write two or three chapters, but gave up when the scenario became a reality. One of my daughter's friends, a young, beautiful violinist sitting at the back of the second violins married a young, charismatic conductor of one of the London orchestras. Actually the real reason I stopped was that Mills and Boons wanted a scenario for the rest of the book, with all the ups and downs demanded by any romantic fiction, before ending in "happily ever after". I hadn't worked all that out because it seemed obvious that all would be well in the end, so what went on in-between was really just padding.

So now, in my usual ignorant way, I have decided to write an autobiography. Autobiographies have not been a genre that I have read a great deal, and I find myself with a similar dilemma. It would be easy to start as Raymond (my husband), would have, by saying, "I was born at a very early age", and then continue with childhood, adolescence, marriage and becoming a successful pianist. When I did read autobiographies I was always fascinated by the childhood and growing up period, but once the writer's ambitions had been fulfilled and a list of successes followed, I would lose interest completely. So, my decision is that I will only write about my life up to the age of 19 or 20.

Writing about myself immediately points up the questions, "Who am I, and Why am I?" And that brings us back to the age-old nature versus nurture debate, genetics and environment. How far back is it relevant? Is there an historical memory? Jung thought so and there have been times in my life when I was convinced of it. Because my forebears were immigrants and not distinguished in their time, there is little or no information about them before the 19th century. My mother's family was from Latvia and Lithuania and my father's from Poland. Curiosity about ancestors seems to be quite a modern phenomenon. In earlier years nobody asked any questions to fill out the tales they were told, so myths and magic surrounded these wandering Jews. For instance, my father always said he came from Lodz, but on further investigation, it seems that it was not Lodz, but a village, or small town, about 60k from Lodz. So there are probably stories about Rosa Salkinder, my maternal grandmother, which have been embellished over the years, but she was a truly remarkable woman and the fountainhead of an extraordinary family.

First Movement

Exposition

Lineage

Working Woman - Coloured drypoint

Retired Man - Coloured drypoint

My Maternal Grandparents

Rosa Salkinder

Hillel Brenner

Just before her sixteenth birthday, in 1905, Rosa, her parents and two of his sisters (three of thirteen children), set off from Tuckums in Latvia for the distant land of Africa where they intended to set up home, leaving behind the virulent anti-Semitism and political unrest of Europe. Latvia at that time was part of the Russian Empire and although the small town of Tuckums on the coast, (not far from Riga, the capital), had escaped incessant pogroms, there was a notable occasion when Polish boys, who had just been enlisted into the Russian army, got very drunk and burned down a number of wooden Jewish homes. Rosa and her family would also have been aware, to some degree, of the political ferment in Russia. 1905 saw the first

Russian revolution which was put down by the Tsarist army, but I wonder if any of the Salkinders knew that South Africa too was in turmoil, just recovering from the violent Anglo-Boer Wars. For Rosa it must have seemed like a great adventure, setting off to a country which she knew next to nothing about. She did know that she had relatives there and that a cousin would meet them at the station when they eventually arrived in Kimberley. But first they had to pack all their belongings including, to her delight, the very important feather beds. To add to the excitement they would be spending a few days in London, somewhere that didn't seem to be too far away. When I knew her as my Granny, she never talked about her life in Tuckums but told the story to anyone who would listen, of her ride in an underground tube-train in London.

Leaving London they were back on a ship. This time it would take weeks before they landed in Cape Town and transferred lock, stock and barrel to a train to take them to Kimberley, the diamond-mining town in the exact centre of South Africa. The journey would take them over green mountains, and then endless hours, many days, of uninteresting, uninhabited, desert land. Did she know that she would never see snow again, and possibly never again be near the sea? And it would have been difficult to image how different the climate would be. She had never known temperatures higher that 24 degrees and, although Latvia was cold and snowy in winter, they had stoves which heated their houses. In Kimberley It would be very hot (often reaching 40 degrees), dry and dusty in summer and desert-cold in winter, especially at night when the temperature could fall below freezing and the only warmth would be an occasional paraffin heater.

They were not coming to a quiet peaceful town, but one which, until five years earlier had been under a five-month siege during the Anglo-Boer War (1899–1902). Cecil Rhodes, the governor of South Africa, had been determined that Kimberley would remain British and that his investment in the diamond industry would not be taken over by the Boers (the original Dutch settlers of South Africa.) So he had hurried to Kimberley from Cape Town, and set up defenses which held, but which inflicted near starvation on the inhabitants. (The siege was lifted on 15 February 1900, but the war continued until May 1902.) The British eventually won this war but by foul means. The huge British army could not defeat the Boers who were fighting a guerrilla war, so they instigated a scorched earth policy, burning down the Boer farms and imprisoning the women and children in the first ever concentration camps, one of which was in Kimberley. The inadequate shelter, poor diet, lack of sewage and overcrowding led to malnutrition and contagious diseases such as measles, typhoid and dysentery. 30,000 people died, 27,000 of them children.

My grandmother and her educated, middle class family would not have had any idea what awaited them. The city had a dissolute atmosphere: drinking dens and brothels dominated the sleazy Wild West desert mining town. There were however, some grand buildings, such as the City Hall, a club built for Cecil Rhodes and the other diamond moguls like Barney Barnato and Sammy Marks. There were about six hundred Jews in Kimberley in 1876 and a magnificent synagogue was built, but after gold was discovered in Johannesburg in 1886, most of the Jewish population moved there.

At long last, the train bearing the Salkinders reached Kimberley station and Rosa leaned out of the window and caught sight of her cousin, Hillel Brenner, who was waiting on the platform to greet them. She was 16 years old and instantly fell head over heels in love with him.

Hillel, who was born in Lithuania in a village called Pokroy, had been in South Africa for some years. He had wandered around from town to town trying to find work, and had changed his name from Klavinski to Brenner, as had one of his brothers in America. I have seen some of his registration papers: everywhere he went, or perhaps every year, he had to register his details including his occupation. All the papers have different occupations: tinker, tailor, butcher, baker, whatever. However, he had landed up in Kimberley and was on the station to meet his relatives. He was tall dark and handsome - every young girl's fantasy. By the time I knew him he was bald and always wore a hat, but I am sure that at that time he had enough hair to complete the picture. He passed on his good looks and his height to his children, who were all taller than average for people of their generation.

As Rosa was so young when this romantic meeting took place, her parents were against the relationship she was so eager to develop. Hillel's brother, the one who had emigrated to America, had become a very rich and successful business man, but Hillel was much less motivated or ambitious, and Rosa's parents were not enamoured, so it was some years before they finally gave their consent, and the two were married.

In the intervening years Rosa, who had been educated in German, learned to speak English and Afrikaans and, like all well brought up European girls, painted and probably played the piano. I never heard her play, but as three of her daughters and two of her granddaughters became pianists, (my sister and I carrying on the tradition), I'm sure the genes and the interest started with her.

After Rosa and Hillel's marriage, life took off in a different direction. They become the owners of a corrugated-iron General Store in Cape Town Road, Beaconsfield, with living space behind the shop and a large yard. Beaconsfield is a suburb of Kimberley and did not have the disreputable atmosphere of the centre of the town, but the environment was inhospitable, bleak, open, scrub desert ground. It was, however, near the railway station. The railway was vital because it had recently opened up Kimberley to Cape Town and Durban. Later it meant that my family, living in Durban, could visit, even though it was a 23-hour train journey.

Looking at pictures of Beaconsfield today, it has become even more desolate and neglected, but there was a period when it had a vibrancy and energy created largely by Jewish immigrants who built up businesses, wrote books, played music, danced and partied.

Over the years the Brenner family increased. They had five living children and the yard behind the house became filled with animals: geese, chickens, pigeons, cats and dogs. At one time they had a cow which enabled them to made and sell butter, cheese and milk. Remarkably Rosa became expert at looking after everything. The house, food, animals, the shop, even midwifery, and later she developed an eye for beautiful furniture and ornaments.

One of my most abiding memories is of my Granny in her yard, her housecoat wrapped around her and a chicken under her arm. She is feeding it some tit bit.

"What is the matter with the chicken?" I asked.

"Its sick, it's got the pip," she answered.

For years I truly believed that she was just using the phrase in the human sense. "The Pip" was a phrase used to mean, in modern slang, "feeling pissed off" as in, "I've got the pip". It could also just mean not feeling too good, but astonishingly, I have just learnt that it actually is a chicken virus and that the expression originated from a disease which had been passed from chickens to humans. Rosa was never to be underestimated.

She obviously loved her chickens, but it didn't prevent her having them killed in the yard. They were there to provide food. A *schochet, (a religious Jew who is licensed and trained to kill animals)* would come to her yard and swiftly cut the chosen chicken's throat. The poor dead thing would run around headless, flapping its wings. It's a gruesome sight. Why didn't it just drop down dead? I had nightmares of beheaded people flapping around my bed.

Hillel, my grandfather, was never seen in the yard but spent a great deal of time sitting on the stoop (the verandah) in deep silence. However, he did make vermicelli (lochen in Yiddish). First he made a pasta dough, then a white sheet was spread over the table, and on it he would knead the dough until it was flexible enough for him to start stretching and pulling it. When it was so long that it hung over the table, he would fold it over and over and then cut it evenly and paper-thin.

Hillel's silence and immobility were a mystery to me and so I asked my mother, "Why is he always so silent and still?"

"He's ill," was her answer.

"What's the matter with him?"

"He has polyps in his nose".

"Really? Can't he have them taken out?"

"He doesn't want to," she answered, closing the conversation.

She was always loath to name illnesses, and it was likely that he suffered from malaria and heart disease.

Rosa was a wonderful cook. I remember her once, on the eve of the entire family descending on her, standing in the kitchen, the outside temperature around 40 degrees, sweating profusely over the coal-fired range and cooking five different dishes, the favourite food of each of the five children. It was all traditional Russian/Jewish food, using a lot of chicken fat or cream, and it was delicious. Chicken soup was invariably on the menu.

Once the chicken had been killed and plucked, the innards had to be removed. Any bits, which were inedible, and there were few, were dropped to the animals waiting at her feet. The resulting soup was unforgettable. It contained many intriguing fragments of chicken: innards, stomach, neck, tiny yellow balls (unfertilised eggs), globs of chicken fat and, most important, Hillel's lochen. It was not appertising to look at, but was delicious. Excess fat from the chicken was rendered down and the resulting crackling, called gribenes, was eaten with bread. Rosa would cut slices of bread from a large loaf tucked under her arm, sometimes buttering it before slicing it. Another delicacy was marrow from large beef or lamb bones served with salt on bread (now it a sold at expensive restaurants), or blintzes which are pancakes, usually stuffed with cream cheese, egg, and sugar, folded over and fried. There was a variation she made called something like "Salty Noses" (our name for it), which excluded the frying, but instead the blintzes were baked in cream.

So many of these delicious foods are frowned upon nowadays. So much saturated fat!

I spent many of my long holidays in Beaconsfield and

although I loved being with my grandparents and loved the freedom of no school and no parental control, I was not at all happy in the yard of the Cape Town Road house. I had to have my eyes open to the pitfalls, like the sewage hole which had once accidentally been left uncovered and into which my cousin Barry had fallen. Just as bad were the geese. A fear inducing gaggle surging towards me hissing, with necks outstretched, would send me rushing to the safety of the house.

There was no indoor sanitation, the lavatory was in the yard. It was spine-chillingly loathsome. Inside was a seat covering a huge hole. I was terrified of it. It was dark and not only was the stench unbearable, but I was convinced that all sorts of dreadful creepy-crawly things would climb up and bite my bum. I must have had terrible constipation during the time we spent there.

After many years they moved house to Blacking Street. This was a much more comfortable home and had a proper garden. There were still chickens and a cage of pigeons but, fortunately, no geese. A windmill pumped water into a huge steel container and this enabled a series of irrigation trenches that watered a flower-garden, a grapevine, huge sunflowers and melons. There was a shaded stoop for Hillel to sit in and, most importantly, an inside bathroom. The house was filled with beautiful antiques. I think some of them must have originated in Tuckums but others were bought from people who were hit by the depression and needed to sell their possessions. Rosa had amazing taste which did not always appeal to her daughters. When she died, I feared that my mother would discard the outmoded Victoriana and I wrote from London begging her not to do so. Whether my letter make the slightest difference I will never know, but the fact is that all Rosa's grandchildren have items from her collection. However, the Pre-Raphaelite prints adorning her walls with their rather risqué titles did not survive.

Her sewing room was piled with cloth from the shop and had a treadle sewing machine which I learned to use. She had boned corsets in there, hers, which were patched with multi-coloured scraps and hung up on the wall like a collage. She was a round lady, who became larger with age and these patched, boned corsets must have been agony to wear, especially in the heat of Kimberley.

"Why don't you get a new corset?" I asked.

"They are much more comfortable than the new ones," she told me.

In those days no respectable woman would go corset-less.

There was also a harmonium in that room; a small reed organ with foot bellows to pump the air through the reeds. Fun to play. Many years later, in London, I earned a little money playing such a harmonium at a synagogue for Saturday morning services.

The Shop

It was called a General Store and that is what it was. It sold everything from bicycles and tools to cotton-cloth and sweets. Rosa was not only the general factotum, but also the beating heart that made the shop a success and the centre of social life for the rather poor inhabitants of Beaconsfield. Grandpa Hillel was squirreled away in an office somewhere at the back where he could remain silent and still.

I loved being in the shop. It was dark, and had areas which were mysterious. I never ventured into them but stayed near to Granny while she chatted to her customers in Afrikaans. She would often be measuring cotton cloth, which she had pulled out onto the counter from the shelves that were laden with bales of flowery printed material. Sweets were kept in large glass containers in full view, and there seemed to be no limit to the amount of sugar mice or jelly babies I was allowed. Jute sacks on the floor were filled with flour, rice and beans which rippled though my fingers as I ran my hands though them.

In the front of the shop the road was sand and the pavement was sand - red sand. Everything was sandy. Sand storms swept across the desolate landscape, sometimes they arrived as mini tornadoes. You could watch the funnel of dust sweeping towards the town. There was very little rain, but that too came in the form of storms. Windswept rain-drops thundered on the tin roof.

Despite her never-ending tasks and the difficulties of every day life in a foreign country, Rosa brought up all her children as if they were in Europe. No mean task, because, although there were some good schools, the prevailing population of Afrikaans farmers and miners were not geared to further education and careers, particularly for women.

Frieda, the oldest daughter, became a schoolteacher and taught in the villages outside Kimberley.

My mother Gertie became an outstanding pianist and piano teacher with many students.

Uncle Joe later ran the business but he had learned the violin, like all good Jewish boys.

Ethyl was an amazing musician. She had the imagination and the ear to improvise beautiful things on the piano. Very romantic and dreamy. Very like herself.

Ida, who was a late arrival in the family, was also a very talented pianist. She later ran the Piano Teachers' Association in Johannesburg.

Strangely, it was only my sister Lorraine and I who carried the musical heritage into the next generation.

As well as being educated, the Brenner girls were also dressed in the height of 1920s fashion. These clothes allowed the women much more freedom than previous fashions. A straight-line chemise topped by a close-fitting cloche hat or flattened hair. Low-waisted dresses with fullness at the hemline allowed them to literally kick up their heels and dance the Charleston. Later the fashion was for a boyish look. Straight up and down. At this point my mother told me that she had bound her rather voluptuous breasts flat so as to fit the silhouette.

Just before I left South Africa for London, I visited my grandparents in Beaconsfield. Although neither of them were very old, she in her 60s, I had a premonition that I would never see them again. That came true, as she died aged 62 of pleurisy.

At that point Hillel lost the will to live and needed constant attention. The daughters took it in turns to live with him and nurse him for some weeks at a time, neglecting their own husbands and children. I thought it was cruel, he didn't want to go on living without Rosa, and all the medication, injections and resuscitations were to prove useless, and he died about a year after her.

Rosa and Hillel's wedding

Three Aunts And An Uncle

All the Brenner family (c.1943)

Back row - Ida, Ethyl, Joe, Gertie, Frieda
Middle – Grandpa Hillel and Granny Rosa
Bottom – Anthya, Lorraine, Milton, Barry and Ghita

Frieda

My mother Gertie, her brother and three sisters were an exceptionally close-knit family. As the years went by they were separated by hundreds of miles and later, when my parents emigrated to London, it was thousands of miles, but their emotional attachment continued and was passed down to their children.

Aunty Frieda was my mother's older sister, the eldest sibling, fourteen months older than Gertie: tall and slim with fair hair and blue eyes, a look which was not appreciated when she was young.

"Like a bean pole," was my mother's judgement.

However she was very bright and well educated and was a schoolteacher before she married. She would tell stories of the poor country folk she taught in small villages outside Kimberley. My favourite was about the very dirty urchin she sent home one day with instructions to wash himself. The next day his mother came storming in shouting,

"My Jimmy ain't no rose. Larn 'im. Don't smell 'im".

She had all the typical attributes of the oldest sibling, always in charge, very bossy and demanding and therefore quite frightening to her nieces and nephews. But then she had been a schoolteacher and so always insisted that we behave ourselves.

It must have been humiliating for her when my mother, her younger sister, married a year or two before she did - quite an unusual situation in those days. However, it was not too long before she found a husband, Harry Blumenfeld, a gentle giant; even taller than Frieda; quite a lot older than her; and as quiet as she was excitable.

He owned a bakery in Brakpan, a gold mining town on the Reef, not far from Johannesburg and they set up home at 59 Rhodes Avenue. This became the heart of all family occasions, the centre point between Durban and Kimberley, and near enough for all the extended family to visit.

We didn't see a great deal of Harry because he spent nearly all his time at his bakery, leaving before the crack of dawn and therefore needing quiet early nights. But in his giant-like way he would appear at parties in time to have his photo taken, smiling gently.

Frieda and Harry had two children, my cousins Barry and Ghita.

Barry was an exceptionally energetic and excitable boy and in Frieda's eyes, badly behaved, naughty and unmanageable. I remember her chasing him around the dining room table, stick in hand, furious, ready to beat him. Fortunately for him, he was faster than she was and got away.

I think he must have missed his father's presence, but, luckily for him, they had a wonderful servant, Joseph, a middle aged black man who stood in as a father figure and sometime protector. We all loved Joseph, who not only ran the house, but had time to play games with us when Frieda was not there.

Barry was definitely hyper-active and would possibly these days have been diagnosed as having ADHD (Attention Deficit Hyperactivity Disorder). Once when he was about 10 or 11, staying at our house in Durban, he disappeared one morning and returned and hour or so later, red, hot and sweating, having run down the steep hill to the race course, round it, and back up again. Letting off steam. Quite a feat.

There are family stories which seem to float around in the atmosphere. I snatch at them. Perhaps they are true, perhaps they have been novelised over the years. I did hear, however, the sisters talking around my bed when I was presumed to be asleep during my holidays in Kimberley, and there are other stories which have been dropped into conversations, perhaps unintentionally. So the story of Ghita's birth may be one of these.

Barry was only a year old when his sister arrived rather unexpectedly.

Frieda always said that she was completely unaware that she was pregnant. One day she felt the urgent need to shit and she rushed to the lavatory. To her amazement it was not faeces but a baby that was emerging from her body - the baby Ghita, who was only just saved from being born directly into the lavatory bowl. Not only was Ghita a wonderful surprise, she was also picture-book pretty: blond curls and big blue eyes. A treasure, and Frieda treated her as such. Although intelligent and educated, Frieda was, like her sisters, very superstitious. Her mother's Latvian influence was still strong, and as it is said, "You can take the girl out of Latvia, but you can't take Latvia out of the girl".

So Ghita wore an amulet of garlic and other noxious substances round her neck to ward off the evil eye and we were told that we were never to praise her beauty or anything else about her. I was quite jealous of how exquisitely dressed she always was and I was therefore tempted to mention how good she looked to see if an evil witch ould descend.

Harry died many years before Frieda, who lived into her nineties, becoming less fearsome, gentler and very proud of her extended family. She kept a scrapbook she called a "nachus" book (Yiddish for pleasure and pride). Any nachus-making events from any of her nephews, nieces and their offspring were stuck into the book. This pride in her family helped cement us together. Although scattered to the furthest corners of the world, all of we cousins are still in contact and meet whenever possible.

Joe

Uncle Joe was my mother's only brother, the only son, and was therefore adored, and to some extent spoiled, by all the women in the family. He could easily be described as tall, dark and handsome, but he was not a *dashing* tall, dark and handsome, rather he was a quiet, religious and extremely kind man.

When I was visiting my grandparents before Joe was married, I noticed that every morning he "laid tefillin". Tefillin, also called phylacteries, are a set of small black leather boxes containing scrolls of parchment inscribed with verses from the Torah . He would wind the black leather straps around his arm and attach the boxes to his forehead and arms, wrap his white tallis with its fringes over his head and around his shoulders and, swaying back and forth, intone the morning prayer. Of course he attended synagogue every Friday night and Saturday morning, not to mention all the High Holy Days. He was a genuinely religious person and the regular rituals suited his character.

Later in his life and until his death he was in charge of the Chevra Kadisha, the Jewish Burial Society, which is a voluntary organisation of Jewish men and women who ensure that the bodies of the dead are prepared for burial according to Jewish tradition. It is considered a great blessing to do this.

One of the whispered confidences that I heard when I was supposedly asleep, was that because Joe was such a "good" boy: shy and retiring, not one of the crowd at the tennis or boating or dancing parties and still a virgin at an age where it started to worry his mother, she arranged for him to visit a prostitute. Of course it was never mentioned, but were they all worrying that he could be homosexual? It is hard to imagine a mother contemplating such an arrangement, let alone carrying it out, but Rosa did it. Nothing was beyond her.

And then, when he did fall in love with a respectable young woman, she did not measure up as a wife for the adored son and brother. There are stories about this too; I overheard the murmuring.

"She's an assistant in the shop!"

"She isn't Jewish."

"She's not pretty, rather the opposite"

"She's too poor."

Who knows what else?

So, although this caused him much unhappiness, he was not strong enough to withstand the pressure from the powerful women in his family and was persuaded to let her go.

Eventually, when his was thirty-five he married Minnie. I liked her very much, but she still did not please his sisters. They always found something rather spiteful to say about her even when she gave birth to a son, Leslie, and a daughter, Beverley. I didn't know either cousin when they were children because I had already left for England before they were born.

Joe became the owner and manager of the family shop, and was well known and loved in the neighbourhood, especially by a large numbers of poverty-stricken men and women. Once a week he would give them enough money to keep them going for a few days.

A genuinely good man.

Ethyl

Aunty Ethyl was the third Brenner daughter, the forth sibling. Like her sisters, she too was beautiful, but with a much gentler, quieter appearance. There was always something romantic about her, which was apparent when she played the piano. She didn't attempt the great and dramatic classics but would sit at the piano and, letting her fingers roam around unfettered, improvise beautiful sounds.

She was very young when she married Gabi Freedman, a tall, dark and handsome young man, probably fitting her romantic image of her knight in shining armour.

They went to live in Krugesdorp, another mining town on the Reef. Unfortunately, her romantic dream was not fulfilled. There were always money problems and an obnoxious mother-in-law to contend with and, although this was never openly mentioned, Gabi, seemed to me, to be a very violent man who physically abused his son Milton.

At one time when all we cousins shared a room, Milton kept us awake by banging his forehead continually on the pillow, and also sitting in the bed, rocking himself back and forth with such vigour that it moved across the room. The sisters, discussing this over my assumed sleeping body, decided that he had adenoids and had difficulty breathing. Of course at the time I didn't know that these were well-known psychological symptoms of distress, but I knew that he was not a happy child. When he grew a little older he also dirtied his pants long after it was excusable and he smelt terrible. I once saw Gabi beating him because of this, and then putting him under their house in the dark as a punishment.

However, Ethyl loved Gabi and was lost when he died of a brain condition, maybe an aneurism. The story that I heard was, that during army training, he had accidentally been hit on the head by a dummy hand-grenade, and that he suffered from that for the rest of his short life. His death shocked and grieved everyone. Ethyl's future was a great cause of anxiety. She now had two very young children and was virtually penniless. How was she to manage? How could a single young woman be expected to bring up a son, without a man around?

My father offered to adopt Milton, he would have loved to have a boy in the family, but that was seen in those days, and in that old fashioned town, to be totally unacceptable. Certainly Ethyl had no intention of losing her son, so she returned home to Kimberley and eventually it was arranged, that she would marry Solly Ginsberg.

She was renowned in Kimberley for her beauty. When she was only 17, she had been chosen by Edward, Prince of Wales, to be his dancing partner for the night at a ball organised to entertain the future King during his Royal Tour of South Africa.

Solly Ginsberg was not someone with whom she had ever envisioned spending her life. Solly had always been a presence in Beaconsfield and we children loved him because he had a car with a "dicky", in which he would take us for rides, (the dicky was a folding outside seat, the third seat in the back of his old-fashioned two-seater car) but he was not Ethyl's equal in any way, not as educated, not romantically inclined and was physically short and sturdy with a strong Russian accent. In every way the opposite of Gabi. But he was kind and gentle and became a wonderful father to her children, always considerate, sympathetic and generous. This must have played a huge part in helping Milton become the loving, gentle, helpful man whom all the family love.

Ethyl was still very young and beautiful and she had married Solly for security and as a father for her children. She didn't love him and from what I gathered from the sisters' secret murmurings, sex with him was out of the question. So during the long, sad, lonely years she had a secret love affair. Her best friend was her black maid, and between them they kept the secret from her husband, her parents and probably from her children.

Ida

My Aunty Ida was only eight years older than me; the youngest sibling of the Brenner family. The fact that I always called her "Aunty" Ida didn't strike me as ridiculous until I was a young teenager. I had many "Aunties" who weren't aunties but my mother's female friends, and "Uncles" who were not uncles but the husbands of the aunties. The time arose with all these uncles and aunts when, as an adult, on more or less equal terms, it was both an embarrassment to continue with the prefix, and an embarrassment to stop using it.

However, with Ida it was easy. She was a friend, a kindly elder sister. My daughter wore her daughter's outgrown clothes and her son was born one year later than mine. We were six thousand miles apart, but the bond that bound all the Brenner family together was as strong as ever, and, in 1986, when I was in deep despair about my daughter's near-fatal illness, she flew over at a moment's notice to be with me.

I have no memory of seeing Ida around her parent's home when I was there during holidays in the 1940s. She didn't come with us to the family farm and certainly didn't join in with her little nieces and nephews in the "shows" we performed.

But of course, she too was on holiday, her school holidays,

and she spent most of them in Brakpan with her sister Frieda and her friend and cousin Anita, thus avoiding the disruptive children invading her home. When she was a little older, she visited us in Durban and my mother "fished out" young Jewish service men who might make good husbands for her beautiful young sister. And she was beautiful; very tall, with dark curly hair and the perfect figure. She didn't fall for any of them although, a little later, she did marry a serviceman, a dashing paratrooper, Nathan Vogelman, whom she met in Brakpan.

She was an excellent pianist and must have started on her teaching career whist very young. As far as I can discover, there was no school of music available for budding young musicians in Kimberley. My mother always told me that she herself had had a wonderful musical education from a nun at her school. So perhaps music teaching was quite intense during the time the girls were in the later years at school, thus enabling them to pass strings of performing and teaching exams before they left.

Aunty Frieda met Ida's future husband in a bank in Brakpan. At this time Aunty Ethyl was a young widow with two children and Frieda, with marriage in mind, invited Nathan to dinner to meet Ethyl. When he arrived, he was surprised, and somewhat shocked, to find two beautiful young women present. He always said that he fell instantly in love with Ida - he wasn't going to burden himself with Ethyl's two small children - but it took months before he plucked up the courage to ask Ida out.

He part owned and ran the Park Hotel in Brakpan. During the war, as a soldier, he had been very badly wounded in Greece, but he was now fit and well and retained a very macho attitude to life. This made him a very successful hotel keeper, especially in the bar. Although he was Jewish, he was uneducated and uninterested in the religious aspects of life but, being a good South African, was very interested and educated in sports.

This rather "rough" side of him excited the quietly brought up twenty-two year old girl from Beaconsfield and in 1947 they were married. I was their bridesmaid and remember the joy and happiness they had that day. Dancing on the tables.

But now Ida had to drop the music side of her life and help run the hotel. To me it is inexplicable that she thought that she could no longer go on teaching the piano. I know that it was expected of wives in those days, to give up their careers on marriage, but it was only six years later that I married, and it never crossed my mind that I would no longer play or teach. However, music still meant a great deal to her and she become involved in the Music Teachers Association and continued as its secretary for many years.

Both she and Nathan worked at the Park Hotel, living there until their first child was born when they moved into a house. Nine years later they bought another hotel in a small mining town, Stilfontein, and moved into that. Ida and Nathan had three children: Gail and, after a series of miscarriages and almost nine months bed rest, Rozelle. Later, Lloyd was born. Life was not easy for Ida as she became more and more involved in running the housekeeping and restaurant of the hotel, which she did with super-human energy and efficiency. But it took its toll and she had a breakdown. She had given up music, which had been so important to her emotional life, and things were not wonderful in her marriage. It was a marriage of opposites. After a time she recovered and, in later life, Nathan and Ida were devoted to each other, especially when they retired from the hotel business, bought a pretty suburban house and lived quietly in Johannesburg. With a piano.

My Mother And Father

Gertrude Brenner   Cyril Isadore Israel

Gertrude   **Always known as Gertie**

Writing about my mother is, in many ways, the most difficult part of my story. Although I never felt relaxed and happy about our relationship, I have realised in my old age, that I owe almost everything in my life to her. This would seem obvious, after all she gave birth to me, but because of her ambitions for me, and her determination to see them fulfilled, she shaped my whole life.

She was not open about her own life, and told me very little about her early years, so the best description I can give of that period of her youth is contained in photos, and the little she did say about her childhood. She was the second of six children and was only fourteen months younger than her elder sister Frieda. She always said that they were treated as twins, but I don't know what the difference is between being treated as sisters or twins. I think she never wanted to be considered "the second" and maybe this created her will and ambition.

Gertie and Frieda

This lovely photo is of the two girls at about two or three years old. They were very different, Frieda being blond and rather plain, and Gertie, dark and pretty.

Gertie talked about herself as being a sickly child, having very fragile health. She told me that she had had all the childhood illnesses and, in addition, the dreaded scarlet fever one after another, ending with an operation to her ankle. "What was that for?" I asked. She couldn't remember.

Logically, if she had all those illnesses her siblings too must have had them. They were crowded together, probably sleeping in the same room and even in the same beds. I don't think this entered her consciousness, in the same way that the death of her 14-month-old sister Pauline, when Gertie was eight years old, seemed to have been wiped from her memory. It wasn't until some years after her death that I learned of the existence of Pauline, when Aunty Frieda decided to put up a gravestone for her in the Kimberley cemetery. So the remaining siblings then consisted of Frieda, Gertie, Joe, and Ethyl and much later Ida. Ida was sixteen years younger than my mother.

Despite all the illnesses, Gertie survived and grew into a stunning "flapper" style girl. The photos show her with her sister and friends at boating parties and tennis parties, dressed in the most up-to-date 1920s clothes. Very Scott Fitzgerald without the money or the booze. How they managed this, 6.000 miles away from Europe and 10,000 miles from the USA, boggles the imagination. I can only imagine that magazines would come their way, and that they themselves, or perhaps a dressmaker, would copy the latest fashions.

Later in her life as styles of dress changed, clothes continued to look wonderful on her. She had an ample bosom (now unbound), very slim hips and thighs, and no bottom to speak of, which meant that whatever she wore always fell beautifully. She wasn't at all extravagant but, because of her shape, she looked stunning in anything she wore.

I know that in her childhood she had to help in the mini-farm in the back yard of her home, as well as in the family shop, but she was very bright and very talented and was soon flourishing as an outstanding pianist and teacher as well as playing the piano for the silent movies.

At the age of 21 she married my father, Cyril Isadore Israel, always known as Issie. He was 31 and, as both families lived in the small suburb of Beaconsfield, they had been friends for most of their lives. He was an inch or two shorter than Gertie, but had a muscular body and thick black hair and the two of them made a very attractive couple. I wonder if she knew when she agreed to the marriage, that she was going to leave home and move to Durban,

Gertie and Issie

I think she would, in any case, have given up working immediately on marrying, as was the custom in those days, but she had also moved away from Kimberley to Durban, and after a honeymoon, (she told me that it was on a cruise ship) they lived in a hotel until their house at 23 Coronation Road was built.

She was very young, and had left her very close-knit family and her friends and pupils, and moved to a city, more than 600 miles away, where she had to make a new life for herself. Here there was good news and bad news. The good news was that Issie's brother Solly was already living in Durban and that could have been the making of a new family connection. But Solly's wife Beth and Gertie never became friends. That family was our only relatives in Durban, and it was unfortunate that the two women were so different and so antagonistic.

However, Gertie was a very resourceful woman. She was only twenty-one and basically on her own in Durban. Communication with her family was very difficult and very expensive She must have missed her parents and her siblings and the help they would have been able to give her.

So now she had to learn to run a home, cope with servants, help her husband in his business and make new friends. And when her children came along, train them to fulfill the plans and ambitions she had for them. However the small Durban Jewish community welcomed Gertie and Issie, and the friends they made there, remained loyal even after they came to live in London.

They had very little money in their early years and were not averse to having lodgers. A number of young male immigrants stayed at Coronation Road, and most of them eventually succeeded brilliantly in the businesses they started. By the time I came along the lodgers had disappeared and were never mentioned. Gertie was very ambitious and therefore somewhat snobbish, so having been a landlady was banished from her history.

Back in Kimberley she had not had a conventional European-type music education. There was no Conservatoire or Music Academy but she had been to a Catholic convent school where it seems that one of the nuns was an outstanding music teacher. Not only did my mother leave school with a string of performing and teaching diplomas, but an academic understanding of the music she learned. Her book of Beethoven sonatas, which I still have, has penciled analytical notes explaining the almost mathematical structure of the music. She loved Beethoven and rated him above any other composer. In her opinion, he never wrote anything which was not perfect. Quite honestly, I don't think that at the time she had heard a lot of music; she told me that on first hearing Debussy, she thought it was discordant and ugly. Nowadays, I feel like that about music by Stockhausen.

I don't know if she sat at the piano and played through her beloved Beethoven when she was on her own at home. Possibly she did when I was very young, before the war took over all her time, but sometimes she would play to my sister and me. We always begged for Schubert's Earl-king which thrilled and terrified us; the piano part of this song is particularly difficult with the constantly repeated chords, imitating a galloping horse ridden by a father holding tight to his little son whilst fleeing from "death" who wants the boy's life. At the end death wins, the child dies. We also loved her to play the Beethoven "Waldstein" sonata, one of his most difficult pieces. Like most children I took it for granted, perhaps all mothers were amazing pianists, and it took me many years to appreciate what a talented musician she was. She was in many ways more wide-ranging than me. She was a brilliant sight-reader and able to morph into popular music when it was needed for the shows she produced during the war and on board the ship bringing us to England.

We didn't have a lot of sheet music in the house but there was a series of blue-bound books - Folio Edition - of miscellaneous pieces of music presumably produced for amateur pianists to play for their own pleasure and to entertain their family and friends. Most of it was too difficult for me as a child, but, because Gertie played them so beautifully, it became a source of serious ambition for me, and I had lots of fun picking out tunes or reading the lyrics of the songs.

I could not have been more than eight or nine when it was arranged that I would play the Mozart C major piano sonata at a student concert that my piano teacher (Dorothy Patterson) was putting on. Someone had discovered that Grieg had written a second piano part for the sonata, so my mother and I played it together. It was the only time I remember playing with her. Even at home, we never played duets.

Gertie had an absolutely non-tactile approach to child rearing. I have a very clear visual memory, back stage after one of my very first concerts with the Durban Symphony Orchestra, of being surrounded by giant adults, and peering out between them at my mother at the back of the room, nowhere near me, not saying anything and certainly not kissing me or telling me how proud she surely felt. I learned to know that if she said nothing, she was pleased with me. I had to be contented with that.

Lorraine, me and Gertie

She also made the mistake of "putting" both my sister, who was three and a half years younger than me, on the piano. It is not unusual for siblings to play duets and two-piano pieces professionally, but it certainly didn't work for the two of us. It would have been so much better if one of us played a different instrument, because I always felt that Lorraine and I were in competition with each other, and my mother did nothing to placate this. In fact, I think she thought that it would spur us on. It didn't. It separated us. Didn't encourage friendship. I had the strong belief that Gertie favoured Lorraine, and I was jealous. She would point out how long Lorraine's legs were, how she was going to be tall and slim, (wrong, she is very slim but a few inches smaller than me), how she took after the Brenner family in looks whereas I looked like my father (this was not a compliment).

It has remained difficult for me to know whether my interest and need to succeed at the piano was purely my own, or how large a part of it was a wanting to gain approbation from my mother. How else was I to achieve that? But I think I was deeply fascinated and moved by the music I played and I didn't object to spending hours at the piano. My sister was different. She had to be forced to practise. I have a letter from my mother to me when I was in London telling me how well Lorraine was doing,

"I don't even need to hit her any more".

Wow!

Despite this, Lorraine became an excellent pianist, studying from the same teacher in London as I did, and had the beginning of a very successful career, but she couldn't see a long-term future as a pianist and, after marrying, turned to music therapy and later became an eminent Doctor of Psychology.

My mother was a very complex person, very volatile, very moody, the opposite of my father who was always stable and reliable. She had grown up poor and, perhaps because of that, and because she was very bright and very talented, she wanted a fulfilled life, which for her meant having money, friends and having brilliant, beautiful children who could realise these dreams for her.

Appearances mattered enormously. When I was about six, I was a flower-girl to one of her friends. I had just lost my top front teeth, a very normal occurrence, but she gave me strict instructions that when photographs were being taken I was not to smile. "Keep your lips together". She was already trying very hard to turn me into the picture she carried in her mind.

My relationship with her was never as close as I would have liked it to be. I think I started having feelings of irritation with her as an adolescent when any questions I asked would be met with clichés. For example: she didn't understand why my sister and I fought so much.

"After all you are sisters". End of discussion.

The fact that she hung back when I was growing up from any verbal praise or physical expression of my achievements, or my appearance, left me unsure and introverted. Even more upsetting was her constant nagging of my father. He seemed oblivious of it, but I hated it.

Gertie developed serious, chronic asthma in her thirties, when I was about eight years old, and that became the priority in all our lives. No one seemed to known how or why she developed this disease, but without the medicines they have today to treat asthma, she seemed often to be at death's door.

Over the years many causes were held responsible. The Durban climate, with its high humidity choking the air was the first to be blamed - we would go and stay for short periods up country to the fresher hilltop breezes. There was a time when we went to Kimberley for a few weeks. The extreme dryness was worth a try. The Frangipani tree overlooking her bedroom, with its exotic cream and yellow, powerfully scented flowers, was chopped down; perhaps it was the pollen she was allergic to. And then the brown bread which, was all that was available during the war, could have been the cause. She bought rye flour and that was made into bread but nothing made any difference. She went on coughing and choking.

My father, angelically, took care of her during these attacks, but it did mean that she was the only one allowed to be ill. If I woke up in the morning with a cold, or any other complaint, he would turf me out of bed. I did have measles and whooping cough, and I certainly suffered frequent bouts of tonsillitis, but I think that must have been before my mother became so ill. Her asthma is so ingrained in my memory that it is hard to remember that, between the attacks of asthma, she was a healthy young woman and able to take care of her children when they were unwell.

As the years went on allergy tests became available and they pointed to all sorts of foods, so after some years it seemed that she was virtually not eating anything. After my parents came to England in the 50s they would often go to Switzerland or the French Alps to clinics which promised help. I think they both enjoyed being in these lovely places and returned with advice on even more foods to give up. Extraordinarily, there was even a time when smoking was suggested. It was considered very healthy then. Finally, in the 1960s, cortisone was discovered, and this kept her alive until she was seventy-four.

Cyril Isadore Israel   Always know as Issie

My father Issie was four years old when he left the village near Lodz (Poland), where he was born. He had no memory of those very early years, beyond the fear instilled into him by his parents, of the constant attacks against Jews by the Cossacks, something that had been happening for hundreds of years. The Russian Cossacks would storm into small settlements on horseback and pillage, rape and slaughter all in their wake. So, in fear of their lives and knowing that even if they survived the attacks, the Russians, who were now in power in Poland, would enlist all boys aged 12 to serve for 20 years in the Russian army, they escaped. Anyone who could, fled. Millions emigrated to find a safer, better life, amongst them my father, his parents, and his four siblings.

Issie's father's name was Meir Krokocki but later he changed the family name to Israel, the given name of his father, because people struggled to pronounce Krokocki. He was married three times. His first wife died after giving birth to two sons, Solly and Harry. Meir's second wife Sarah had three children - my father, his sister Gertie and the youngest son, Lawrence. This was the family who left Lodz that day in 1904/5.

Somehow they arrived in London, only to be met by the news that they could not stay, not even for a short while. Because of the waves of immigrants arriving at the end of the 19th and beginning of the 20th centuries, Britain had imposed a strict quota for Jews, and so Jewish organisations had been set up to raise money to dispatch those unwanted immigrants. They were put on ships leaving London as quickly as possible - any ship. Many people realised their dream of going to the USA, the golden promise-land, but others found themselves on the way to diverse distant parts, and my family were on their way to South Africa. Perhaps the thought of a new peaceful and prosperous life kept them content on the long boat trip but they would have no real knowledge of the land to which they were headed. They probably landed near Cape Town, and there, people would have told them of the diamonds and the growing wealth of Kimberley, hundreds of miles north. So that is where they went, and that is where they settled, starting a general store which grew big enough over the years to feed, clothe and educate the family.

By the time I arrived on the scene, none of them lived in Kimberley. My uncles and my aunt had moved to more promising areas of the country. Sarah, my grandmother, had died in the 1918 flu epidemic and Meir had married again for the third time. My father never told us what happened to his stepmother. I presume she too had died which left Meir wandering from one of his children to another. He did come and stay with us in Durban at one time but that didn't last long. I don't think my mother had much time for him. The thing I remember most about him, really the only thing I remember of him, was that he had very bad nosebleeds. We were told that it was caused by his excessively high blood pressure.

So, although I saw a great deal of my mother's family in Kimberley during my childhood, I had no connection with my father's, not even with Issie's half-brother, Solly, who lived in Durban with his wife Beth and their two children. My mother and Beth didn't get on at all. Gertie thought Beth was stuck up and unfriendly so, although they were our only relatives in the city, the only relatives for hundreds of miles around, we had virtually no contact with them. I hope Issie saw his brother on his own but he never spoke of it. Beth became a figure of fun; she carried her head tilted in the air, nose upwards. Maybe it was genetic, or perhaps she had developed this posture. There was at that time an advertisement for Bisto gravy powder. The people pictured always had their noses in the air - sniffing the delicious aroma of Bisto gravy as it wafted past. "Ah-ah." Hence, Beth became Mrs. Bisto.

It seems reasonable to believe that Issie had a happy and healthy childhood. He grew into a happy and healthy man. He was not academic, his talents lay in other directions. He was not a reader, had terrible trouble with spelling, but he was brilliant with his hands: understood cars, mechanics, repairing things, building things. He was probably dyslexic, a gene which, it is possible, has passed down the generations. But not being academic gave him the freedom to be an adventurer, a sportsman, and freed him from being a typical Jewish wimp. When he was 14, at the outbreak of World War 1, he ran away from home and tried to join the air force; a very un-jewish, daring adventure. Of course, he was turned away. He could hardly have faked his age because he was very small. He never grew tall, he was about 5ft 5" as an adult, but he was well built, muscular and strong. His happy home life was shattered however, when his mother died. Issie was 17 years old when the Spanish Flu epidemic hit South Africa. This devastating pandemic killed approximately 20 million people worldwide (half a million in South Africa), and was unique in that it was the strong healthy people who died, suddenly and without any previous symptoms. This is what happened to Sarah, Issie's mother, but Issie was convinced that it was not a virus which caused the tragedy, that she had died from eating cucumber. She had eaten a lot of her favourite Polish pickled cucumber with her dinner one night and by the next morning was dead. He was not superstitious, had no ritualistic customs, but he believed with all his broken heart that she should not have eaten the cucumber - that it had killed her. So he swore that no one he loved would ever even taste the poisonous vegetable. We never did.

Sarah Israel

After her death, his father married again and, for my father, this wife epitomised the wicked stepmother in all the fairy tales. He never expressed any particular reasons for his hatred, so it might just have been the distress of someone taking the place of his beloved, beautiful mother.

Perhaps he needed to escape from his no-longer happy home, and living in South Africa gave him the opportunity. For although his desire to become an engineer was thwarted by the need to help run the family business, he did find some freedom and fulfillment as the traveling salesman. In one of the many cars he owned over the years, he would set out into the undeveloped and inhospitable country to sell goods to the Boer farmers. Their six-thousand-acre farms were isolated, only connected to each other by rough wagon trails.

During the Boer War, the British had burned down most of the clay, thatched, two-roomed Boer farmhouses. Although they had been rebuilt and the farms had been regenerated, the people were very poor and mostly badly educated. But Issie was a man who could get on with anyone, and always spoke of the friendliness and generosity of these people who lived in a completely alien world to his Jewish trading family. The roads he travelled on were dust tracks, but in this semi-desert, when it did rain, the dry riverbeds he had to cross turned to mud. There is a photo of his car being dragged out of one of these mud rivers by a team of oxen. For him this was freedom and excitement, and he continued, during his life in South Africa, to drive long distances on virtually unmade roads.

Fortunately for me he was a keen photographer and this has given me a picture of his life before I knew him. There are photos of hunting trips, rugby tours (he dislocated a shoulder playing rugby and suffered arthritic pain later in life), of river parties, tennis parties, lots and lots of different cars draped with women, and photos of trips around the Cape. Being the adventurous spirit he was, in 1926, when he heard of the possibility of a new diamond rush taking place about 200 miles north of Kimberley, he set off to try and make his fortune. I always knew that Issie had taken part in a diamond rush. He had told us stories of how he had prospected for diamonds: how he walked the site looking for the most likely place to dig, lined up to run when the starting gun was fired and then ran to peg out the area he thought most promising. With the help of a number of men, usually black, they would then dig and dig and wash the gravel; rejoicing or despairing with the results. During his time there he took a wonderful series of photos which are truly historic and, luckily, he had written above many of them the place and the date where he had taken them. A lot of the photos mentioned "Bakers," "Bakers Main Street" or "Dealers at Bakers". I was intrigued and did some research. Where and what was Bakers, sometimes called Bakersville?

This is what I discovered.

In 1924 Koosie Voorendyk was digging a cattle dip on the family farm called Bakers when he saw a glitter in the gravel and picked up the glittering stone. He took it to his science teacher who put it through an acid test and declared that it was a 3 carat diamond. That is about 9.5 mm in diameter.

Immediately his family invited the state geologist and prospected PR Hager to the farm. He was unimpressed. "My boy," he said, "There are no diamonds on this farm. A bird must have dropped it".

Hager himself then went on to prospect various farms in the district until having got lost he found himself back at Bakers where he found a huge 6 carat diamond - 11.7 mm . Within days he had found 360 diamonds and in 1926 a "rush" was announced.

Almost instantly professional diggers, fortune seekers and adventurers arrived and by 1927 Bakers (now called "Bakersville") had a population of 150,000 diggers and their families and 250 diamond buyers. It became known as a "city of shacks". Houses and shacks stood wall-to-wall for several kilometres It even boasted cafes, a cinema, shops and other businesses and at one point had 17 schools; one of them had 15 classrooms. During that year and the next a phenomenal amount of diamonds were found just beneath the topsoil.

By 1928, two years later, the rush was over. Everything and everyone had disappeared. Only a few foolhardy spirits remained, sifting though the gravel in the deserted dust bowl.

I was really excited to find that my father had played a small part in such an enormous event. I don't know how long Issie stayed there. I'm afraid he didn't make his fortune and so had to go back to the family business. He did, however, miraculously dig up the diamond that became my mother's engagement ring. The ring is beautifully set in gold and platinum with the actual 1carat diamond surrounded by diamond chips. My mother wore it all her life and after she died I inherited it. It was the only thing of hers I really wanted to have and I never take it off, it has such strong emotional significance for me.

Issie(right) with diamond

Issie was 31 when he married my 21year-old mother in 1931 and moved to Durban. I think he really enjoyed his bachelor years but was deeply in love with Gertie, a love that was obvious for the remaining years of his life. They honeymooned on board a ship which took them round the coast of South Africa and then moved into a hotel whilst their house was being built. The move to Durban, or at least away from Kimberley, was necessary because the family store had burned down, and for some unknown reason, the insurance had not been renewed. Life had to start again. Brother Solly had already settled in Durban and he must have convinced Issie that here was a good place to start his new life.

Durban, a small seaside resort, did not offer Issie the excitement of life in Kimberley, but it was a growing, up-and-coming town. Because of the large, deep harbour, the whaling industry and coal exporting, it was becoming an important industrial site. Although it was still very small, beautiful Art Deco buildings were being constructed, and there was a small Jewish community, so it could offer a newly married man a good place to raise a family. In many ways it was as foreign to him and my mother as Kimberley was to Poland. For a start, the climate was the extreme opposite. Kimberley, in the middle of South Africa, as far inland as you could go, was semi-desert: very dry, very hot summers and very dry, cold winters. Durban was subtropical, very hot, very wet, very humid, with not much difference from summer to winter. Durban is at sea level; Kimberly's altitude is 1200 m (4000ft). My mother's family would now be 600 miles away. In those days roads were often unmade, trains were extremely slow and telephone calls difficult and very expensive. It could well have been a different country.

I was born two years later in 1933 and my sister in 1936. They were now installed in the house that was my home for seventeen years. Friends have told me that in the very early days, perhaps even before I was born, they had lodgers. Whether they were paying lodgers or just young immigrant men from Europe with no money and nowhere to stay, I don't know. My mother never mentioned them and neither did Issie, but he told me that he had given Mr. F, who had become one of the richest men in South Africa, his first £5.

He was a warm and loving father. I can remember him brushing my long blond curls when I was a tiny girl and he continued all his life to be very close to me. Although (as was the custom) he never actually told me he loved me, I was always aware of his love. I think it would have given him great joy to have had a son, or at least to have a daughter who was athletic, rather than a moody musician. Nevertheless, he was obviously proud of my musical success. He tried to strengthen my flabby muscles by lifting me up to hang on one of the branches of the avocado-pear tree in our garden and encouraged me to pull myself up. He must have been so disappointed at my feeble attempts. However I did manage to stand on my hands with my feet balanced on a wall, do cartwheels, and I enjoyed being wheeled around while walking on my hands.

He rarely lost his temper. Years later I asked him how he managed to do that. He didn't reply. I thought that my mother constantly nagged and bickered at him. In retrospect, I can imagine that that was how their relationship worked and I wonder if he was even aware of it. He truly loved her and I admired him for his constant attention to her, even when it meant being up at night when she had asthma attacks, making tea, rubbing her back and generally trying to help.

For someone who was so easy-going, when he did lose his temper he was almost out of control. I was to discover this one morning.

I hated walking to school in the heat and humidity and that morning I nagged and nagged him to drive me to school in the car. He was unusually irritable, and wouldn't do it. Something else must have upset him because, suddenly, he lashed out and hit me. Did not beat me, just smacked rather too hard. My shock was so great that I didn't go to school at all, and he spent the day, phoning home from work to see if I was OK. This was the one and only time it ever happened. It seemed to be completely out of character, although I seem to remember him screaming at someone outside our house one evening in that out-of-control voice.

His Shop

It was called "Worths" and was a long, narrow, two-storied building right between the classy, Art Deco big stores such as Payne Brothers, John Orr's and Stuttafords. The first two-thirds of the ground floor were devoted to "Mens Wear". This didn't include suits, jackets or trousers, as off-the-peg clothes hardly existed in those days. There were, however, bales of fine suiting material to choose from and tailors working on the upper floor to make them. My father, using his engineering skills, would measure the men downstairs, and the tailors would cut out and make up the suits. When the customer returned, my father would make sure the suit fitted him perfectly, adjusting the shoulders or length of the sleeves and sending it back upstairs to be finished to perfection. The rear of the ground floor was partitioned off and became a barber shop - so any customer could leave Worths perfectly fitted out, shaven and coiffeured.

He went to his shop every day except Sunday, when he usually played golf in the morning. Much as I loved him, Sunday lunch became a trial whilst he went through his golf card and discussed every shot in great detail. The Durban golf course debarred Jewish members, so he would have to drive down to Isipingo, a town on the coast, south of Durban where they welcomed any white man. Sometimes the whole family would go (my mother also played golf) and he taught me how to hold the club and how to swing it, encouraging me to keep my eye on the ball, but that's as far as it went. I had to spend too many of my Sundays practising the piano for some upcoming event or other.

I remember with special affection the rare occasions when we went out together, just the two of us. I tried to enjoy the rugby matches he loved, but it was not really my scene. Once or twice I went with him when he visited his suppliers in Johannesburg. I disliked Jo'burg. Durban was green and hilly and had the sea, Jo'burg was a big city, full of tall buildings, and bustling dirty streets, but to be taken and introduced to his business friends was memorable.

He belonged to a Masonic Lodge and this caused us to tease him a lot. My sister and I had discovered the special bag with the secret regalia.

"We know," we said, "you take all your clothes off, put on the little apron and ride round on goats. Fun".

"Ha ha! But really we do a lot of charitable work, which is the most important thing."

I believe that, in reality, it gave him an opportunity to meet people who were useful in business and with whom he would otherwise have had no contact. Because of the experience and knowledge he had gained on the diamond diggings, and the contacts he still had with diamond dealers, he was occasionally asked, probably by his fellow masons, to find them a diamond. He loved to show me the little folded tissue paper which, when opened, would contain a sparkling array of diamonds of all sizes. He would keep the packet in one of his pockets and would excitedly ask if I wanted to see them. He was always very quiet and almost reverential when he put on his jeweler's eye loupe, opened the packet, and explained about the size (measured in carats), and the colours and their purity or otherwise.

"Look," he would say handing me the eyeglass. "Can you see that back spot? That will reduce the value and the beauty."

I found it hard to see.

"And the blue ones are the best."

He never quite managed to enthuse me about diamonds, but not only did he find them beautiful, he knew that diamonds are easy to take with you when you are driven out of a country.

There was a time when he was to become the Master mason but in order to achieve this, he had to learn from memory, in order to perform some sort of rite, pages and pages from a little book of mysteries. This actually was very difficult for him and my mother would sit with the book of mumbo-jumbo and prompt him. We were all delighted when he finally achieved his objective and went back to enjoying life.

When he didn't have to memorise words, he loved performing. My parents' best friends, the Geshens, had a farm which we used to visit, and their son David reminded me of the New Year's Eve party at the farm, when Issie, dressed as a woman with a baby, was getting married, shot-gun style. He also made the most of his role as Neptune in the ritual of "crossing the line" on the ship bringing us to England. So, perhaps my performing gene was not just inherited from my pianist mother, but also from my actor, comedian manqué father.

When he and my mother immigrated to London, he became very keen on DIY and made the built-in wardrobes in my bedroom. He also took an interest in gardening. This got him out of his flat and into my garden. The problem was that the gardening he understood in Durban was the opposite of gardening in London. In Durban any plant or cutting which was popped into the soil, would immediately root, sprout and probably flower. He was very disappointed to find that in London every plant has to be nurtured, fed, watered and would lose its leaves and probably disappear for ever. However, he really enjoyed using secateurs and redesigning the roses. After my parents bought "Pannels Ash," a 16th century thatched cottage with three acres of ground, he found the perfect place to spend his energies.

Unfortunately, he only had a few years to enjoy this rustic idyll, as he had a stroke whilst he was at Pannels Ash. It took some days, too long, for it to be diagnosed but when he got back to London he was rushed into hospital, had an operation to drain blood and appeared to have recovered. However, the damage to his brain had a weird outcome. He was completely unaware that he had lost a quarter of his sight on the left and was furious that he was not allowed to drive any more. He had also lost the ability to put physical things in the correct order. For example, in which place to put cutlery when laying the table and, in the days before duvets, whether the sheet went on top or underneath the blanket. Even more disturbing was that this calm, tolerant man would now lose his temper and get very angry at the drop of a hat. He only outlived the initial stroke for about 18 months before suffering another stroke which, this time took his life.

Issie, in a beautiful car outside his home

Burned Shop

Honeymoon

Issie and brother Solly outside "Worths"

Second Movement

Divertmento

Childhood

First Steps - Oil on canvas

Prelude

Me aged three and a half

I am sitting on a stool in front of a piano. The piano is a huge wooden beast with black and white teeth stretching out on either side of me, much further than my arms can reach. The fingers of both my hands are grouped over a few of them. Behind me stands my mother. She is teaching me what the teeth are called. Sometimes she calls them keys and sometimes notes.

The black dots in the book I have propped up above the keys, also has notes. They have names from the alphabet, and when I see one that I have learned is C, I have to play the key on the piano which is also called C. Its fun, but quite difficult.

Mummy is pleased with me because, with my fingers curled over the teeth-keys, as if they were holding little balls, and with one finger moving at a time, I have just finished playing a tune.

"Good," she says. "Get up darling, I will play your piece for you."

So we change places.

The piano is not too big for her. She can reach all the notes and stretch her fingers over at least eight of them. She plays a lot of them together. It's a wonderful sound. Then she plays my piece. But it is not exactly my piece. It has more notes, lots of extra frills and her hands run up and down so fast that I can hardly see them.

"That's not my piece," I shout. "I'll never be able to play that piece."

"Yes, you will," she answers. "I promise you that if you do lots of practise every day, you will be able to do it."

I am confused and sad. It's too difficult. But in my heart I really would love to play like that, and I know that if I ever do, Mummy will be very pleased with me.

So every day I sit at my place in front of the piano, with mummy helping me, practising.

As the years go past, this is where I spend much of my time and where my mother's promise comes to fruition.

Earliest Memories

Me with Mummy

Trying to recall my first memories, I realise that they are like snapshots, just a second in time where a picture comes to mind. And sometimes it is difficult to differentiate reality of memory with an actual photo. Those snaps of the little blond, curly headed girl in beautiful dresses smiling in her mother's arms; playing with the dog; the home movie of the child running in the sunken gardens on the beach front at Durban. Do I actually remember any of those things or are the photos so deeply sketched into my mind that they have become the memories?

My very first memory was being told that I was going to have a new baby brother or sister.

I was three years old and I was standing in the back of our car behind my Mummy and Daddy.

I wanted a brother and assumed that I would get one. He would look like one of the little boys in a picture book I loved. My second memory is of the day the baby arrived. My grandmother Rosa had come from Kimberley with her youngest daughter Ida, and Ida's cousin Anita, and it was arranged for the three of us to go to the park for a little while. When we came back Granny rushed up to us, all excited and said,

"The doctor has brought you a new baby sister".

I was very curious about how that had happened.

"He brought her in a suitcase", she told me

Of course I didn't understand why the doctor had brought a girl when I had ordered a boy. Disappointments in life begin very early.

I have very upsetting memories of the cruelty my sister and I received from some of the nannies we had as small children.

Writing this memoir I find again and again, that along with the sadness of losing my parents, is the frustration of not being able to question them about the mysteries of my childhood.

Why didn't we have a Zulu nanny, for example? All white middle-class South African children had nannies, and I seem to remember the native black women being kind and loving to their charges. We had "coloured" (mixed race) women who were not kind and loving.

The reason could have been that my mother was born and brought up in Kimberley where there were few "native" black people. The original people of the area were San (Bushmen), migratory people who were virtually wiped out by the white farmers. Most of the black people working in the mines in the area were immigrants from other parts of Southern Africa. There were however, a lot of mixed race people known as "coloured". Before the British had installed themselves in Kimberley, before diamonds were discovered, the area was called West Griqualand, and was inhabited by the Griqua people. They are a mixed race because of the intermarriages and sexual relations between the Dutch colonists in the Cape and the Khoikhoi (Hottentot) living there in the 17th and 18th century.

When my parents moved to Durban they knew nothing of the multitude of Zulu people who lived there, and it is possible that they were, therefore, not inclined (probably frightened), to leave their children in the care of these very large, very black people. So our Granny sent coloured women from Kimberley to Durban to be our nannies.

It was a mistake. When my mother talked of the blond

curly hair and long eyelashes I had as a very small child she always told the story of the nanny who had cut off my eyelashes. I don't remember that, but do remember the time when, as a punishment, my sister was pushed into a wicker laundry-basket and the lid firmly shut. I tried unsuccessfully to release her but had to run off to find someone else to do it. Lorraine is still quite claustrophobic. Perhaps it stems from that incident.

My most vivid memory is of walking through a park with my nanny who pulled a stick from a tree and beat me on my bare legs. I couldn't have been more than 4 or 5 and it seemed that she was very angry with me for taking, stealing, a pencil from her room. Like all bullies, she made me swear not to tell my parents or she would inflict even more and worse punishment. It was only when my mother discovered the welts on my legs that she learned what was going on and the evil witch was dismissed.

Disappointment. Gertie, Lorraine and me

Life In Our House (and other houses)

Coronation Road (Lorraine at the Gate)

Our house looked like a child's drawing of a house without the chimney, and with windows only on the right hand side. On the left, it had covered verandahs (called stoops), one downstairs and one upstairs. From the downstairs stoop, steps led down to the garden-path with a lawn on both sides and flower-beds flanking the stairs. The picture was completed with a surrounding garden filled with trees and flowers, and a yellow sun in a blue sky. In our back garden we had two avocado-pear trees, both producing huge, buttery fruit. The best avocados in the world. We also had bananas, paw-paws and mango trees, and a hedge of guavas screening the small rooms (called kayas), where our African servants lived.

The house was on a steep hill and on the left hand side, the floor was about four feet off the ground and not bricked in, but had three or four arched openings. The one nearest the front of the house was later excavated by my father and turned into an air-raid shelter. If my sister and I were brave enough, we could creep into the other dank, scary caves. Usually that would be for a dare, because it was dark in there and infested with creepy-crawly things - poisonous spiders and scorpions. We certainly never stayed there more than a moment or two and would tear out into the light, and onto the driveway leading to the garage.

Huge red poinsettias and pink hydrangeas on the other side of the drive formed a hedge between our house and our neighbours. A hole in the fence behind the flowers enabled us to slip through to play with Joan, the girl in the house next door. Her house was much like ours: two-storied, "Modern," and brick-built, but our neighbours on the other side, lived in a building that was all corrugated iron.

My parents were not real friends of either of these neighbours but across the road, in a bungalow, lived Mrs. Henry. Our family was very friendly with Mrs. Henry. She would invite my sister and me in for tea: a proper English tea, with orange squash, cucumber sandwiches, scones and cake. Unfortunately we couldn't eat the cucumber sandwiches (my father had banned cucumber), so after the first time, she put some sort of fish paste on the bread. One Christmas she gave me a present of a colouring-in book. This was the first and only Christmas present I had ever been given. Being good Jewish people we didn't celebrate that festival, but this gift enabled me, when school restarted after the holidays, to talk proudly of my present, instead of sitting in embarrassed silence when everyone was asking, "What did you get?"

Besides having the biggest hydrangeas in the street, she also had had two grown up sons, one of whom was good looking and the other not. I decided that I really liked the younger good-looking one because, when he got into his car, he drove off almost immediately. He didn't tinker about, the way his older brother did. I don't remember getting to know them; they were so much older than me. I just watched them from our balcony.

After some years it seemed that we needed another bedroom (it was a three bedroomed house): perhaps my grandfather, (my father's father) would be moving in, so my parents built an extension to the back of the house. I loved the excitement of the imagined newness and the smell of the cement. Now there were four bedrooms and mine was the brand new room with built-in wardrobes and a washbasin in a cupboard. There was only one bathroom in the house so this was a luxury. Grandfather never came to stay with us for any length of time, but would come for short periods and then move on to one of his other children. He was, by now, a widower for the third time. He was paunchy and bald and spoke with such a strong Polish accent that I don't remember ever talking to him, but I do remember his massive nosebleeds. He would sit in a chair with a blood-soaked towel held on his thrown back-face.

The morning-room, which housed the upright Steinway piano and a dining table and chairs, was under my room This is where we ate every day, the official dining room having new, black, extremely elaborate furniture where dinner parties were held. Neither my sister nor I were ever at the dinner parties. In those days children were to be seen and not heard – except for piano recitals. As a result of the new build, there was a large porch leading from the garden to the kitchen. It was here that my father built an aviary and started breeding canaries.

"Why are you doing this?" I asked him,

"I hate birds in cages. They ought to be flying free."

"Canaries have always been bred and lived in cages so they have never known anything else," he told me."Don't you think they are beautiful? I am going to breed the best singing canary in the world!"

He was leaving producing the best pianist in the world to my mother. I have no idea what happened to those bird prodigies but I don't think they were for sale; it was merely a hobby.

,,,,,,,,,,,,,,,,,,,,,,,

Up the steps from the front path of the house was the stoop, open to the side and the front of the house. The perfect place for taking family photos. The front door opened into a hall, with the staircase on the left and the sitting room on the right. Many of my adult dreams feature this hall; it seemed to be full of secrets and is still vividly in my mind. The phone was on a shelf in the corner and behind it was "under the stairs". A small storeroom.

Under the stairs was a brilliant place to hide and eavesdrop on the telephone conversations my mother had with her friends. She spoke very often to Minnie, her best friend. She had a way of talking to her that I found annoying and upsetting. I had the impression that Minnie was very patronising towards my mother, and that my mother accepted this and was obsequious to her. Although it would be strange if this were true, because Gertie was a feisty woman and their friendship continued even after Minnie emigrated to Israel and Gertie to London. Probably I was jealous. I thought she was much nicer to Minnie than to me.

Minnie, her husband Issie, and their three children, (the Geshens) were a lot richer than us, but they were the closest thing we had to family in Durban. We spent many hours playing with David and Myra, the two older children, more often in their house than in ours. David had a wonderful electric-train-set with enough track to go from one room to another. Each of us was stationed in a different room and we sent toy goods and people on the train from one room to another.

One day we decided to put on a show in their sitting room which was in two sections, making it possible to divide the room and rig up a curtain. We had to have two stage managers to cope with opening and shutting it. I still have a programme that we printed, and sold to invited friends and family for three pennies, quite a respectable sum in those days. The money went to a charity. The show started with a play we concocted between us called "Patience". We thought we were very clever because it was about a patient school teacher, trying to control the children in her class who were playing patience (the card game), and not getting on with their work. I see that not only did I co-write the little play, I produced it and played Miss Jones, the teacher. (I must have been a bossy brat.) This was followed by piano solos and poems, and after the interval - Bioscope.

Bioscope is the South African word, still used there today, for cinema. In those days, with no television, showing films on a screen from a projector was a treat. My father would show us Charlie Chaplin silent movies as the entertainment at birthday parties.

We had wonderful Passover nights at the Geshen house. Huge parties, a lot of fun, especially as we were allowed to drink the wine and, as a result, seemed to spend a lot of time under the table. We were also frequent week-end visitors to the farm they owned in the picturesque Valley of a Thousand Hills. These visits took place during the war years when petrol rationing was enforced, and so my Dad tried to find the route with the fewest miles, so as to use the least amount of petrol. More often than not it turned out to be a hidden dust track. His endeavours often ended with a farmer with a tractor having to haul him out of the mud.

I was definitely not a country girl at heart and didn't like trying to sleep in a room in deep darkness, and I was scared of the large insects whirring and flapping around my head. However, I did get the chance to ride a horse, although I think riding is an exaggeration. I sat on the calm, large animal whilst it walked slowly in the spectacular countryside.

....

The sitting room in our house had sofas and chairs around the walls, and our grand piano took pride of place. I spent many, many hours in this room, practising on the Broadwood baby grand. The radio was kept in this room and this is where we would sit quietly listening to the news. It was all war news, and for a long time it was all bad with a covering of uplifting propaganda. I asked my father,

"What was on the news before the war?"

He thought for a while, "Good question", he said

We did own a gramophone but had very few records. They were not produced during the war because the shellac they were made from, was used in the manufacture of arms, but one day my parents managed to buy a recording of Bruno Walter playing the Mozart D minor piano concerto, the very one that I was still studying, and had played with the Durban orchestra. This was a treasure but also a shock. I thought that a recording would be perfect, both in interpretation and certainly in accuracy, but although Maestro Walter was a great conductor, he was not a perfectionist when it came to piano playing. There were lots of wrong notes and technical passages that were far from accurate. I didn't know what to make of this and it remained a bitter disappointment for many years, until l learned how recordings were made, and how almost impossible it was in those early days to achieve perfection.

So, although we had no recorded music, there was some on the radio and I danced, or rather twirled and skipped uninhibitedly in the sitting room. However, there came a time when my mother decided that I should learn ball-room dancing and arranged for the fiancé of the better-looking of Mrs. Henry's sons, to give me some lessons. She was a beautiful ballet dancer and I went across to Mrs. Henry's house for my lessons. The carpet was rolled up and appropriate music played but I couldn't do it. Up close with this unknown person trying to learn the steps and follow her, whilst not looking at my feet - I froze. I never did succeed. It should not have been so difficult for a musician with an inbuilt sense of rhythm, but I felt extremely uncomfortable, never before having had the experience of anyone's arms around me.

....

I am quite hazy about the kitchen. I was not welcome there. It was occupied by our servants, a man called "the boy" and a woman, the "girl". The boy was the cook and the general factotum and the girl was a maid of all work. The boy would not only cook all our food but also their own which consisted mostly of porridge made from mealie-meal and meat which had been boiled out of all recognition. (Mealie is the South African word for sweet-corn). The other occupants of the kitchen were huge cockroaches, about two to three inches long with waving feelers and armour-plated brown bodies. They emerged after dark and could be seen and heard skittering away when the light was switched on. No amount of cleaning or poison made any difference. It was one of the disadvantages of living in a tropical climate. Outside there were flying ants that came in swarms at night-fall. By morning they would have lost their wings and would be wriggling along, tunnelling underground, and transforming into termites. There they would eat at lightening speed through anything buried in the ground.

Our daily meals were on a weekly rota, very boring, and the regularity made it unappetising. There were no surprises, nothing to look forward to. There were times when, as a small child, something like tapioca pudding was served. It made me nauseous even to look it, but the rule was that I would have to stay at the table until I ate it. I remember sitting there whilst the white lumpy mess got colder and colder and more and more disgusting. I couldn't eat it. Eventually it would be taken away, but would reappear the next day. Finally it would disappear, but the memory and the disgust remained forever.

My mother planned the meals and taught the cook, but then it was left to him. Like most white middle class South African Jewish women, she occasionally made a delicious pudding or cake. I have a recipe book from the South African branch of WIZO (Women's International Zionist Organisation) which begins with the desserts. Every other cookbook starts with soup or appetisers. This is the only recipe book I have ever seen like it, and I have seen (and own) many.

In my pre-adolescent years I became quite plump. My mother, the beautiful, slim, elegant woman, was appalled and banned me from eating chocolate, keeping it under lock and key. I wasn't having this treat removed from my life, so I discovered how to raid the sideboard where the chocolate was hidden. It was quite simple. I took the upper drawers out and reaching down to the shelf below, stole the treasure. Obviously my parents soon saw though my burglary act and moved the chocolate somewhere more impregnable. So then I sneaked into the kitchen and made myself chocolate by mixing cocoa power, sugar and water into a delicious paste. But it was not only the chocolate that was locked away. All the cupboards were locked. Everything was locked away from the "untrustworthy native servants". Even the food was portioned out except everyday needs such as tea or coffee and, luckily, cocoa.

....

From the hall, a staircase curved up to a large landing where the continuation of the banisters and spindles created a balcony overlooking the hallway. On the landing there was a very large linen cupboard and a door on the right led onto the upstairs verandah. This was the duplicate of the verandah downstairs but had been screened off with meshing to protect anyone from falling over. When it was stiflingly hot and humid, I begged to be allowed to sleep on the sofa out there. The disadvantage was that it was dark and any light attracted myriads of flying insects, some of which would bite, so a mosquito net had to be rigged up, and I felt a lot safer if I was covered by a sheet.

A door on the left of the landing opened onto a passage. All the upstairs rooms, except my bedroom, led off this passage. So there were three bedrooms, a bathroom and the lavatory. I would get into my room, in the extension, via the usually unused bedroom on the left. Lorraine's room was at the other end of the corridor opposite my parents' room which was a lovely large room with glass French windows opening onto the verandah.

They always slept in twin beds separated by a bedside table. Whether this was because of the heat or because it was fashionable I don't know, but when they came to live in London, they took to the warmth of a double bed. Single beds were all the rage at that time, because in the movies of those days, only twin beds were allowed. Any lovemaking had to be done with one of the actors keeping a foot on the floor. Despite the twin beds, parental sex did take place. Once, when nosing illicitly though the drawers in their room, I came across some condoms. At that time I had no idea what they were. I had absolutely no sex education, so it took quite a long time before I made sense of those little packages. My mother totally ignored the question of sex, but I remember when I was still very young, our maid, who was washing me in the bath, told me about menstrual blood and other things. I was terrified. Much later Gertie must have told me about having periods. I was a very late developer and she became worried that they would never appear, so I was taken to a doctor, my mother's faith in doctors being immense. I was probably given a placebo and, of course, at some point the desired effect occurred. What she completely neglected to tell me was why I had to suffer the "curse".

Even when leaving me, as a 17-year-old, in London, not a word about sex passed her lips. It was fortunate for me that I read so much, because my knowledge came almost entirely from novels.

I think that despite being completely modern as regards clothes and outward appearances, my parents were shy and somewhat innocent. Perhaps innocent is the wrong word, confused and ignorant would be better. Throughout South Africa white men were thought to be friendly, kind and unthreatening, but there was great fear of the uncivilised black man. This didn't extend into the home. Black people lived amongst us and were trusted to look after and not harm us children. They were like domesticated animals, whereas the people roaming the streets were wild and unpredictable and to be feared. I was over protected whilst growing up, especially at night. Walking along the streets during the day was considered safe, but as soon as night fell, the fear of the savage natives emerged and I was not even allowed to cross the road to see a friend without a chaperone. In those days, even before official apartheid was instated, there was a curfew, and black people had to have a pass of some sort to enable them to be on the streets at night.

So, surely parental fear was exaggerated.

Grandpa Meir with me

Minnie and Gertie

Second World War

At the outbreak of World War II in 1939 I was six years old and I was almost 13 when the war with Japan came to an end in August 1945, so almost all of my childhood was overshadowed by it. Of course I didn't know anything about the politics of the country until much later, but it is fascinating to discover what was going on and to realise why Apartheid followed so quickly after the war ended.

On the eve of the British declaration of war against Nazi Germany, on 1st of September 1939, when Germany invaded Poland, South Africa had a coalition government. The Prime Minister was J. B. M. Hertzog, the leader of the pro-Afrikaner and anti-British "National Party". In 1934, they had joined in government with the pro-British "South African Party" of Jan Smuts as the "United Party." The Nationalists under Herzog still harboured a lot of ill feeling against the British in response to their humiliating loss of the Boer War and now wanted to keep South Africa neutral if not pro-German, but as the country was still a dominion of Britain, it was obliged to be on the side of the British. A furious debate took place in Parliament and on 4 September, Herzog was deposed in favour of Smuts. General Smuts (as he was always known) was a great friend of Winston Churchill and served in the Imperial War Cabinet in 1939.

It is also important to know that behind Hertzog was an even more virulently Nazi group, the Afrikaner Ossewabrandwag, a secret society founded in 1918, and dedicated to the concept that *"the Afrikaner Volk has been planted in this country by the "Hand of God..."*

It was *"based on the Fuhrer-principle, fighting against the Empire, the capitalists, the communists, the Jews, the party and the system of parliamentarianism... on the base of national-socialism".*

Members refused to fight in the army and the military wing engaged in sabotage against the government. They dynamited electrical power lines and railroads, cut telegraph and telephone lines and spied on the sea battle outside Durban. The government cracked down on them and imprisoned thousands of them for the duration of the war. Among them was the future prime minister, B.J.Voster.

As I had hardly been aware of life outside my home as a very small child, the transformation of Durban from a sleepy seaside town to one teeming with soldiers and sailors was no surprise to me. I loved looking out to sea from the upstairs balcony of our house at the long rows of ships anchored there. Sometimes there were as many as fifty, all of them shrouded in grey paint except the gleaming white hospital ships with huge red crosses painted on them. They were patiently waiting their turn to dock in the harbour.

The Mediterranean was closed to Allied shipping and so the long perilous journey down the West coast of Africa was the only route to the East and to North Africa. Durban was the best equipped port on that journey. It had the only dry-dock big enough to accommodate a battle-ship, and it was a haven for thousands of the battle-weary men and for those who would soon be in the throes of conflict.

But there was no protection for those ships waiting in convoys at sea. They were immensely vulnerable. The Japanese had bombed and destroyed ships inside the harbour at Port Darwin, Australia. Here they would not even have had to enter the harbour. Many years later a German submarine captain, one of the many who had caused enormous damage to ships further out to sea, said that no one had told them of the waiting convoys. So perhaps the enforced silence about the sea battles that were going on had worked. Few of the residents of Durban knew anything. There were some however, who could hear the German radio propaganda broadcasts which, unfortunately, revealed home truths. There must have been spies amongst us.

The Japanese were snooping around in submarines and when a Japanese aircraft flew over Durban in June 1942, a blackout was ordered for the city. This blackout had its down side; ships couldn't find the port, aircraft couldn't find the landing strips and there were many fatal car crashes. Because the streetlights were switched off and car headlights hooded, they were virtually invisible. One newspaper report said that more people were killed on the road than on active service.

I remember my parents putting up black curtains and keeping them closed at night. Black-out wardens patrolled the street shouting, "Put out that light" to anyone who allowed a chink to escape. Those who were caught breaking this law were taken to court and fined £5.

Later that year things got worse, with German U-boats (submarines) sinking hundreds of vessels, including some passenger ships, on their journey around Africa. As many people as possible were rescued and were brought by the troop ships to Durban. There was a campaign to try to prevent suspected spies from gaining any unwanted information. Posters displaying notices such as "Don't Talk About Shipping" went up everywhere, but it wasn't possible to keep all the bad news secret because it was obvious that, amongst the troops crowding the streets, there were also survivors of those sunken vessels walking and talking amongst us.

When any ship arrived in port, waiting to land, the troops and the passengers must have been amused, but surprised and happy, to be greeted at the dockside by a large middle aged lady, dressed all in white with a big shady hat: Perla Siedle Gibson. She became an icon, known as The Lady In White, and was there to welcome them, whatever the weather, by singing though her megaphone, "Land of Hope and Glory," "Waltzing Matilda" or "The Star Spangled Banner" and all the popular war songs of the day. Later, she wrote of a ship coming into dock, *"her decks crowded with bedraggled survivors wearing all sorts of odd scraps of clothing...anything but downcast, they shouted, the moment they saw me, "Give us a song," and I responded with "There'll Always Be An England". Lustily they joined in."*

She had vowed to sing for every ship that arrived or left Durban and by the end of the war she had sung for over 1300, singing even on the day she heard that her son had been killed fighting in Italy.

The troops who were waiting for their ships to be cleaned and repaired were given a few days leave and housed in tented camps which filled two racecourses, and any other open spaces including one of our local parks, Mitchell Park. This was previously a mini zoo and had housed Nellie the elephant. We all loved Nellie because, not only could she play the mouth-organ and crack coconuts, but we could go for rides on the seats strapped to her back. The Maharaja of Mysore originally presented her to the park in 1928. Nellie left South Africa in 1949 to go to Taronga Zoo in Australia where she was, unfortunately, put in an enclosure with a moat surrounded by a fence. It was soon obvious that did not like this arrangement, and in trying reach over the moat, she broke her back and died.

Besides the camps for Allied troops, there were also camps for Italian and German prisoners of war. The Italian prisoners were allowed to roam around during the day and return to camp at night, but the Germans were never given any freedom. There were also makeshift tented hospitals. My mother trained and became a Red Cross nurse and worked in one of these military hospitals. I have a lovely picture of her with her blue uniform, white starched apron and white starched headdress. One day she told me that she had been reading to a wounded soldier. "Why were you reading to him?" I asked, expecting to hear that he had been blinded in the fighting. "Well, he'd never learned to read," she told me. That was hard for a seven year old book-worm to understand.

The local Durbanites felt it was their responsibility to keep the troops happy, healthy, fed and entertained and did everything in their power to achieve that, to give them a few days ashore which they could always look back to with pleasure. My father would often invite men who shopped in his store to dinner, or take them on sightseeing trips. Local transport, abundant food, and all entertainment was free. Canteens were set up: "Ye Playhouse," a sham Elizabethan tearoom with concrete wooden beams and real mango trees, provided huge steaks, and the Athlone Gardens was open for outdoor dancing.

The Rickshaws, with their Zulu drivers bedecked and painted, were a great attraction, as was the Fitzsimons Snake Park on the beachfront. It had been set up to produce anti-snake venom and contained about 120 indigenous species of snake. The snake handler was a great favourite; apparently fearlessly letting the snakes slither all over him and holding their heads, with open gaping jaws, in his hands.

And then there were the wild monkeys that would appear out of the bush and grab the bananas held out to them. They could bite if they didn't get what they wanted, but the soldiers loved them.

Over the next year or two, wartime became more and more evident.

Of course I had no idea of the realities of it but we did have all the preparations for the real thing. We listened avidly to broadcasts about the progress of the war. So many South African young men were involved in the North African and Italian fields and that was what we heard about most. (We were never told about the war at sea just outside Durban waters.) Everyone had to have an air-raid shelter. My father built one under our house. It was perfect in every way. Shelves of tinned food, electric light and bunks to sit or sleep on. After the war, it was a great place to play in. Air raid sirens went off at random times and we were supposed to go into the shelter and wait until the all-clear sounded. I was always frightened, believing that bombs would start falling. After a time, as this never happened, people started to ignore the sirens.

At school we had to wear dog-tags round our necks for identification as well as a rubber (eraser). The windows were pasted over with white muslin to stop flying shards of glass, and whenever a siren went off we had to duck under our desks and bite on the rubber. We would then be led to the cellars for safety and encouraged to sing rowdy songs to relieve the fear of make-believe bombs.

Towards the end of the war, a number of older English evacuee girls arrived at my school. It must have been a surprise for them to find themselves back in what could develop into another war-zone. They were not as tall as the sporty South Africans and, to my great relief, one of them was even shorter than me. That meant that I no longer had to lead the class around in gym lessons. Hopefully she could understand the strong Scottish accent of the gym mistress that had so confused me.

The Durban Jewish Club was turned over to the British for the duration of the war. Two million men passed through its doors during those years. My mother was very involved there. Not only did she work in the kitchen to feed the men but her ability as a pianist was put to good use, organising and playing at shows for them. My sister Lorraine and I were featured in song and dance items. Gertie made us costumes appropriate for showgirls and we tap-danced, and sang all the popular songs, such as "It's a Long Way to Tipperary," "Hang out your Washing on the Siegfried Line," and "Dinah is there Anyone Finer".

Lorraine, being only about four years old, was a huge success. My father's tailors made her, I remember, a soldier's uniform complete with cap, and the cute little girl, singing and dancing the war-time songs brought the house down. I was very jealous, especially of the beautiful dolls and the dolls clothes presented to her, but at eight years old, I didn't have the cute appeal and probably was a terrible singer.

In 1944 things seemed to be at their lowest point. For us children there was an outbreak of polio and of smallpox. The smallpox was easily dealt with - we all had to be vaccinated. We could choose which arm or which leg we would prefer. I had three scratches on my left leg, which healed quickly. Some people were not so lucky and were left with large scars for the rest of their lives. Polio was a different matter because there was no vaccine and it seemed to strike randomly. My sister and I were never allowed in crowded places such as the swimming pool or the fun-fair at the far end of the beach, as that seemed the only precaution available. Fortunately neither of us contracted the disease. The worst thing we caught was whooping-cough. The cough lasted so long that there was talk of letting us go for a flight in an aeroplane. I'm not sure how that was supposed to help. Anyway it didn't happen and we both recovered.

For the general population everything was in short supply. Petrol was rationed to 200 miles a month. It was a terrible thing to happen to South Africans who loved their cars. That included my father, but for me it was the food shortage that I noticed. I always found the food we had at home boring and bland and, thinking about it now, it could be because it was a matter of making do with what was available. White bread was unobtainable and the replacement brown bread, consisting of wheat bran and vitamins, was virtually inedible. Sometimes my mother managed to get hold of rye flour, and bread was made from that. It was a little better. Meat was rationed. One day a week the butchers shut down. There was even a shortage of fruit and vegetables due to weather conditions. However, there was a flourishing black market and we were told, even if we didn't believe it, of how much worse things were in other parts of the world.

"Eat it all up. Clear your plate. Think of the starving children of.... wherever".

It was during this time that my mother's asthma became the most frightening thing in my life. Her attacks at night were so severe, with ceaseless coughing, that I was sure she was dying. But our lovely doctor would arrive in the early hours of the morning, with his pyjamas sticking out from under his trousers, and give her an adrenaline injection. Suddenly there would be silence in the room. It was so silent that I used to creep to her room and put my ear to the door to try to hear if she was still breathing, still alive. I never had the courage to go in and see for myself and, as I could never hear anything, I would slink back to bed and eventually fall asleep.

It was a huge relief the next morning to find her sitting up in bed in a pretty bed-jacket and lipstick as if nothing had happened.

"If anyone asks how I am darling, just tell them I had a bad headache."

I don't know why she was afraid of allowing herself to mention the word asthma. It was like people not mentioning the word cancer, referring to it as the big C. She was very superstitious and perhaps that had something to do with it; if you don't put a name to the disease it doesn't exist. For years she referred to it as "coughing" but later she called it bronchitis and, because the attacks were always more prevalent after she had some sort of infection, this made sense. In the 1960s when cortisone was first used, she was prescribed huge doses of it. It certainly improved her condition enormously, but the side effects, which were unknown for some years after she first started taking it, had disastrous consequences. I always thought that it had saved her life, but it had also killed her.

Her illness, coming in the middle of wartime undermined my confidence in life and my fears were only intensified when my father, in his usual adventurous way, joined the civil police.

Nearly all the young men had volunteered for the forces leaving a severe shortage of personnel to fill their places. (Of course they had to be white men.) Knowing him, he must have jumped at the chance to go out at night on sorties into the location, raiding illegal beer joints and disarming violent men. After he came home one night, and next morning showed us with pride, a huge knob-kerry - a thick stick with a large ball covered in brass studs, that he had liberated from some drunken man, I became a nervous wreck. On the nights he was out pretending to be a policeman, I was in dire need of comfort and the reassurance that he would return. I don't know whether I expressed this fear in so many words, but my mother, sitting downstairs doing beautiful embroidery, seemed unaware that the loud artificial coughing fits I had, were meant to bring her up to me. Of course she knew about real coughing and wasn't fooled. She didn't come. Cuddles were not in her repertoire.

Despite the feelings generated by this pseudo war, it was only one day, in a building in town, waiting for the lift with my mother, that the reality of it struck home. When the lift doors opened, the waiting people were engulfed by the screams of a hysterical woman. As she staggered out I could make out the words she was frantically howling over and over again,

"He's gone! He's gone!"

"What's the matter with her?" I tremblingly asked my mother.

"Someone she loved has been killed in the war."

Suddenly for me the lift became a place of horror and I couldn't be persuaded to enter it. Surely that was where she heard this terrible news. What would I hear if I entered the crowded space? I couldn't think clearly and was terrified. I let go of my mother's hand and ran.

Gradually the war started to come to an end. The Mediterranean was now open to the Allies and, although there were still troop-ships arriving, the town was less crowded and less vibrant. The shortage of almost everything was, if anything, getting worse: shop windows were almost completely empty, food was even scarcer than before, hotels were not allowed to serve bread after 3pm and the making of toast was outlawed, because it wasted rationed butter!

On May 8 the war in Europe ended and VE Day was declared. There were great celebrations in town. People crowded the streets. Speeches were made, and a variety concert took place on a hastily built stage on the City Hall steps. The town gardens were so crowded with happy people that if you got in, you couldn't get out. I was still too young to take part in this, but when Japan surrendered in August, I went with my family to the Thanksgiving Cavalcade in Albert Park: a gigantic show of military equipment, naval ships, aircraft and goods manufactured in South Africa. My father who was still an ardent photographer, but now with a cine camera, filmed this Cavalcade and also the 1947 visit from the whole of the Royal Family: King George, Queen Elizabeth and the Princesses Elizabeth and Margaret Rose to Durban. They drove down West Street where we watched the parade from the upstairs windows of Worths (my father's shop). He took a lot of pictures from there before rushing off to the Cenotaph to get even more shots.

In 1948, the Nationalist won the election and enforced Apartheid. It was an Afrikaner Party and they felt very strongly that their racial ethnicity should be kept pure. Also many people voted for them because they were fed up with the rationing and shortages caused by the war. As most of the wheat had been sent to Britain (their enemy), a saying went round that, "The National government only got in because it promised white bread". There was some truth in that.

Convoys

The Lady in White

From a postwar magazine – Rickshaw Attraction

Me as showgirl

Holidays In Kimberley

I was 15 years old before we went on a proper family holiday. My parents' volunteer war-work, and the need to make their business successful, took precedence. So, although we had odd weekends away, sometimes even going as far as Brakpan to visit my aunt Frieda and the family, my sister and I were sent to our grandparents for the long summer holidays where our cousins and their mothers often joined us.

My Auntie Frieda's home was in Brakpan and it became the centre point for all the family to meet. We often started our holidays there because it was near to Johannesburg which, for us, was only a thirteen hour train journey (better than twenty-three to Kimberley). Getting from Brakpan to Kimberley - about three hundred miles on an unpaved, dusty, but completely flat road, was comparatively quick.

My father loved to drive us there, and this often turned into an adventure as the roads over the mountain passes were still only glorified dirt tracks. We frequently travelled overnight, and were occasionally caught on the top of a mountain in a thunderstorm. It was terrifying. My sister and I huddled together as thunder, lightening, hail stones and torrential rain thrashed the car, and the road beneath us was washed away. We would have to stop and wait until the next morning when the mud-slides had gone. Issie loved the adventure. I am not sure the rest of us did.

Life for me in Brakpan seemed very bland, but it was the gathering place for the clans. As my grandparents came from families of thirteen children each, there were seemingly hundreds of them. They were a very close-knit family and there seemed to be numerous occasions when they would congregate at Frieda's house. I could never distinguish one from another, but I remember being humiliated by the jovial question:

"Do you remember me?"

I never did, and the standard adult remark to children: "My, haven't you grown?" What did they expect, that I would remain a toddler forever?

I don't have any memorable stories of my holidays there. I was bored. This may be because it always took me at least a day to acclimatise to the altitude. Johannesburg and the towns on the Reef are about 6000ft high and coming from sea level gave me mild altitude sickness. The climate is absolutely ideal, never too hot or too cold, but it does have violent thunderstorms almost every evening at about 4o'clock when monsoon-like rain teems down for about an hour, after which the sun reappears as if nothing had happened. After a week or two, Aunty Frieda would drive us to her mother, our Granny, in Beaconsfield, where we would spend the rest of the holiday.

My Granny's house was full of fascinating things to look at, the yard had its own excitement, and the shop was teeming with people of all colours and languages, but the most exciting thing about Kimberley itself was (and still is) "The Big Hole". This is the largest man made hole in the world. It started life in 1871 as a small hill, but when it was discovered that it was rich in diamonds, thousands of men arrived with picks and shovels. This was the beginning of diamond mining in Kimberley and it continued on that site until 1914.

It is an awe-inspiring sight: one mile wide, and 580 feet deep. Turquoise water filled the bottom and tiny birds darted in and out.

We often went to see it and loved to throw stones down into it to see and hear how long they would take to reach the water. It was futile, the water was too far away, hundreds of feet below.

On the occasions when my mother, Frieda, and Ethyl, gathered in Kimberley, they would sit around my bed at night discussing intimate details of their lives.

These fascinating glimpses into the life of grown-ups were too good too miss, so I lay awake with my eyes closed and my ears wide open and listened to the whispered but heated debates on their marital problems and the difficulties that both Joe and Ethyl were having.

It is strange what sticks in the memory. It must have been in the Blacking Street garden that we children, who were gathered there, climbed into a mulberry tree and picked and ate the fruit. It is a very dark red, and although it would have been quite permissible to eat the fruit, getting our clothes stained certainly was not. So how to clean up before it was discovered? We tried all the washing soaps we could find but to no avail. Then in the bathroom we came across Cuticura hand soap. It seemed to us a very luxurious product that we should not have been using, but to our great relief it removed the stains from our cloths. We created a sort of jingle to this wonder soap. "Cut-ti-cura, cut-ti-cura, cut-ti-cura soap," we sang, dancing round the house. The name has stuck, although I have never used the soap since then.

Members of our huge family, the Datnows, had a farm in the vicinity and we were taken there on many occasions. Although the earth was dry and dusty, this was not an arable farm, when it did rain the smell of the earth lapping up this gift from heaven was never to be forgotten. There were huge herds of cows, whose milk we could drink completely unpasteurised (delicious), and an enormous water tank to swim in. The tank was fed by typical windmills found everywhere in the dry areas of South Africa, not at all like the British or European windmills which ground corn or powered water-wheels, but a circular fan of steel blades atop a tall inverted v-shaped scaffolding, with an extended wing which caught the wind and turned the fan in the right direction. Its sole use was to pump up precious water.

Occasional we were taken on picnics, but mostly we hung around the shop or explored all the intriguing items in the house. There was, of course, a piano, and the necessity to keep practising for the next exam or concert.

By the time I was about nine years old I had become obsessed with Lewis Carroll's "Alice in Wonderland". At that period of their lives, my parents were not great readers, but although we didn't have many books in the house, I must have been read to when I was little because I learned to read very young. Now, I not only wanted to read everything I could get my hands on, but I wanted to own the books I loved. To my parents, owning books seemed a very extravagant luxury, the public library was always there. Luckily, I did own a copy of Alice, which I read incessantly.

Once, on a seemingly endless train journey to Kimberley, I was emersed in my book, when I heard a fellow traveller say,

"Sorry to intrude, but have you got to Tweedledum and Tweedledee yet?"

I looked up at the English officer sitting opposite. It was wartime and many soldiers travelled from one camp to another. I was shocked and amazed. I was unaccustomed to being spoken to as if I were an adult, let alone by one who knew about this wonderful book.

"I still read Alice," this stranger, this alien creature went on, "I love it".

And so we passed the next hour or so discussing the book, the various characters and the strange language. It was wonderful and unforgettable.

I had also fallen in love with theatre. Luckily for me there was a theatre group in Durban and I loved seeing anything they performed. This must have given me the idea of putting on my own mini performances, so I inveigled anyone willing, or unwilling, into joining me in a show. In Kimberley it meant my sister Lorraine and all my young cousins having to learn their parts and take part in a performance of "The Mad Hatter's Tea Party" (more Alice in Wonderland). We rigged up a curtain and, inevitably, the show also included piano solos from Lorraine and me, and any poems anyone knew. My grandparents were the unfortunate audience and I was very upset when my grandfather fell asleep. Later my mother tried to console me.

"He only falls asleep when the performance is good," she said.

I tried hard to believe this deception.

There was a stage of my childhood when I became very prone to tonsillitis. I seemed to live at the end of the "whip them out" time, and it was then considered better to leave the blessed things in the throat causing dreadful pain and illness. It was not until I was twenty-eight, living in London, that my tonsils were finally removed. As antibiotics were only available to the troops in the late 1940s, tonsillitis was treated with sulphonamide drugs. The pills were enormous and they always made me vomit. The other "cure" was painting the tonsils with some noxious brown substance. I could see my enormous tonsils when I stood open-mouthed at the mirror and I would paint the infected spots with a long paintbrush. Usually, after a time, the infection would blow over, but there was the time in Kimberley when this did not happen; it grew worse and I had terrible earache. I remember mutterings of mastoiditis and suddenly I was in hospital. Although I was a young child, parents or family were barred from any visits. I was very frightened. Worst of all, I was presented with tea very early each morning and made to drink it. I had never drunk tea before and it was bitter and full of tannin. It was many, many years before I drank tea again. Even now I drink it very weak to avoid that taste. I have no idea what caused me to recover, probably the thought of the tea.

The Big Hole

Keeping Kosher

Almost all my parent's friends were Jewish and they all kept up the traditions and rituals as we did, but it was not until I met practicing Jews in England and heard about their upbringing, that I realised how "free" we were. Perhaps because we were all spread around the city and around the country, and the sun shone and we were outdoors a lot, that there wasn't the dark ghetto-like intensity which Europeans endured. For us it was as much a social thing as a deeply religious belief.

So, we were a traditional orthodox Jewish family. I would say more traditional than orthodox which means that my parents kept a kosher house, went to synagogue on the High Holy days, kept up the Friday night ritual, and sent us daughters to Hebrew lessons and to synagogue on Saturday mornings. My mother and her family were much more enfolded in their Jewish heritage, but my father took it or left it. He had a barmitzvah but after that I think he lapsed until he married my mother and agreed that they would bring up their children in the traditional way. He read Hebrew very hesitantly but enjoyed the rituals.

We kept a kosher house: no pork or shellfish; no milk products with meat; meat and milk cutlery and crockery kept separate. Meat came from a Kosher butcher where the animal had been killed, prayed over, and drained of its lifeblood. At home it was koshered more. Every trace of blood had to be removed by salting the meat and then soaking it to poor, pale, tough, tasteless lumps. I was fascinated by the method of re-koshering cutlery that had fallen foul of the law in some way, to its former glory. The working part had to be buried in the ground for a certain number of hours.

In honour of Passover, all the crockery and cutlery was changed. Every crumb of food used before that date religiously cleaned away and beautiful, flowered plates appeared for just that one Passover week . We were supposed to walk to synagogue, but it was too far away for us to do that, so we drove. Saturdays were meant for rest and prayer, but my father had to keep his shop open, and I certainly couldn't be let off practising.

Everyone in my mother's family was very superstitious. I remember that when we were traveling anywhere, after the bags were packed, and whilst they were still in the house, we had to sit down, preferably on a suitcase, for one minute before leaving. I have since discovered that it is a Russian habit and appears in Chekhov's "Cherry Orchard". My mother had a superstition that we must never start a project, such as sewing something or making anything on a Friday, and there were numerous superstitious that we children were threatened with. For example; if you pulled an ugly face when the wind changed, your face would remain like that forever; or were caught sitting under a table when a clock struck, you would develop a hump on your back.

This all seemed like nonsense to me, as did the rituals in the synagogue. For years I took the incessant standing and sitting for granted, but one day asked my mother, ensconced upstairs with me amongst the women, what that was about.

"Haven't you noticed" she said, "that you stand when the Ark is open and sit when it is closed. It's a sign of respect for the Torahs inside?"

The Ark was a very glorified cupboard at the eastern end of the synagogue. It was covered by a richly embroidered curtain which was opened and closed by drawstrings, and contained the Torahs, which are scrolls with the laws of God as revealed to Moses inscribed on them. I was beginning to find the whole thing difficult to swallow and was immensely relieved when it was discovered that the only harmony lessons available to me took place on a Saturday morning. "Hurray!" Harmony had become more important than religion. The "hurray" was a little premature because the harmony lessons turned out to be excessively boring. This does indicate that the religious teaching in our house did not go very deep and that is probably why, although there was always a surface of belief, it didn't penetrate my soul, and filtered away from me very quickly.

The social centre for the Jewish community was the Durban Jewish Club. Some of the earliest settlers in South Africa were

Jews. Nathaniel Isaacs who arrived in 1825 was one of the founders of Port Natal, Durban's original name. The attractive old red tiled club was opened in 1913-

"to provide for the Jews of Durban a centre of assembly for the propagation and development of Jewish thought, ideas and culture, and for social intercourse".

"The club was placed at the disposal of his Majesty's and allied forces as a canteen in 1940-1945, and during that period over two million members of the services made use of the premises."

There were (still are) halls that could be used for theatre or musical productions and it is here that I saw the plays which inspired my own "shows". There were also tennis courts and bowling greens, none of which I used, I really didn't mix easily with the young people using the club. I was very shy and refused to join in anything.

"People are saying you are just stuck up," my mother told me. "Why don't you go along and enjoy yourself?"

"How could she not understand?" was what I thought.

Durban has two beaches. The North Beach was just down the road from the Club and therefore the one most Jewish people frequented. Black people were not allowed on the beach. We were told, "Africans don't like swimming. It is not something they do." How convenient! We always went to the North even though I had a feeling that South Beach was much more fun. My parents considered it very down-market. In July all the holiday-makers would go there because it was just at the end of West Street, which was the main shopping road. Many of them would be Afrikaans and not only was there the endemic racial divisions but in our case, there was also a certain amount of snobbery. "We don't mix with the hoi-polloi."

There was always a simmering, underlying anti-semitism about, my school was a prime example of this. Jews were banned from sporting clubs of all sorts. More importantly, the National Party, when it became the government in 1948, had members who were Nazis and almost as anti-Jew as they were virulently anti-Black.

As the war years progressed it became more and more clear to my parents that the Jews of Europe were suffering, although it wasn't until the concentration camps were liberated by the Allies at the end of the war that the real horror was revealed. Even then I knew almost nothing of it. It is amazing how little parents talked to children in those days, or perhaps it was only my parents, besides, I am sure they wanted to protect us from the gruesome reality. As a result of the news of the Holocaust they became ardent Zionists. Not ardent enough to wish to emigrate to Israel when it became a State, but ardent enough to raise money for it in whatever way they could. In my ignorance, I was upset that so much time and effort went into fund-raising for a far away country. The overwhelming poverty in South Africa, our country, the country in which we lived, was simply accepted; we just lived with it and ignored it. It took me many years to realise just how important Israel is to the Jews. At that time, I wanted nothing to do with it.

DURBAN JEWISH CLUB. OLD FORT ROAD. DURBAN SOUTH AFRICA.

Jewish Club

Dorothy Patterson

Dorothy Patterson with Gertie and Issie

Miss Patterson was my first piano teacher in Durban. I have no knowledge of when and how I started lessons with her, or how my mother found her but she was a determining factor in my life. She was over six feel tall and to a small child, she was a huge, intimidating figure with a small head topped by black hair, styled in tight pin curls and corrugated waves. It was thought by everyone who didn't know her as well as I did, that she wore a wig, but as she had a habit of removing one of the hairpins which held the curls in place, and using that to scratch her head, I always felt sure that it really was her hair. The scratching made a strange scraping sound, so distinctive that I can still hear it! Like steel rubbing over sandpaper.

She was an ardent Christian Scientist and told me when I displeased her, and that was often, that she would have to tell her "practitioner" about me. This was a dire warning and I believed that this creature with fiery wings would descend upon me, so I did my best to please her. In reality the practitioner was there to help her with health problems and her understanding of the Bible.

She ran the Dorothy Patterson studios, which were situated in the hall of St Thomas Church. One had to walk down the path behind the church to get to the hall. Her domain consisted of two rooms - her studio, and a waiting room with a table, benches and toilet facilities. I had theory lessons there and I also remember sitting at the table copying out fingerings and dynamic markings from her music to mine. It was very important that these were accurately duplicated because even the slightest deviation from them when I played the piece, would bring down the wrath of the practitioner. Sometimes a slightly different fingering would have suited my hands better and a more personal dynamic could have allowed me to understand the music better, but it was not to be.

I don't know where she had studied. Somehow I remember that she had come from England but otherwise I knew very little about her. She was a single woman who lived in a residential hotel very near to her studio and put her whole life into teaching. She was generally known as "Patty," and because of her size and her hair, was rather a figure of fun. I never ever thought of her by that rather demeaning name. She was always Miss Patterson to me. I wonder if my parents called her Dorothy? It seems unthinkable.

Her studio consisted of a small room decorated in pink. There was an upright piano on one wall. Around two or three of the other walls were built-in boxes covered in pink fabric in which she kept her music, and on the opposite wall to the piano was a window overlooking tennis courts. This small room emphasised the giant size of Miss Patterson. Pink and Miss Patterson seemed totally incongruous but beneath her frightening exterior lurked a bizarre small girl. For example, she had a collection of pencils and rubbers. She sharpened the pencils with a knife to excessively long, dangerous points which could be used as weapons to make sure her pupils' hands were held accurately. As she was always sharpening them they wore down very quickly and when the pencils were about an inch long, they were offered to her pupils as prizes. There were also rubbers, which were rubbed away to become tiny discs. She had names for these miniature pencils and rubbers such as Henrietta and Arabella. I remember her saying,

"If you get it right, you can have Arabella".

A lot of these lessons took place with her leaning out of the window at the back, sharpening pencils and screaming "NO! NO! NO!" I didn't understand at the time how she could possibly know it was wrong without looking at me and, as she never said what was wrong, there were many tearful lessons of repeated mistakes. Besides threatening me with her practitioner she would also yell,

"If you don't get it right you can go and I won't teach you any more."

I was much too timid to try leaving, but my sister Lorraine did walk out, at least on one occasion. I was very impressed.

Her teaching method was for her pupils to learn their given pieces and play them as accurately as possible. There was the inevitable annual Associated Board exams; competitions, (called for some obscure reason, Eisteddfods), held both in Durban and Pietermaritzburg; her own pupil's concerts in the church hall; and, from when I was 9 years old, performances of concertos with the Durban Symphony Orchestra conducted by Edward Dunn. My first concerto performance was movements of the D minor Mozart concerto K466. (I wonder why she chose that particular concerto which is very dark and dramatic.) Later I also did broadcast recitals.

She was very ambitious and took advantage of my talent, and the fact that my mother was equally ambitious, to expose me to the public as often as possible. A teacher only has to have one apparently successful pupil to become sought after.

She had very bizarre rules about the clothes one had to wear at concerts. The dresses were never to be blue (something about the stage lights altering their appearance) and socks had to be dyed in tea so they would not be white and worn with silver shoes. My mother made the dresses so that was not a great problem, but where to get silver shoes for a young child? We had to paint white sandals.

She would always stand in the wings during a performance, unfortunately quite visibly, and commune with her practitioner. It was more frightening than actually playing for hundreds of people.

I was going to school during all those years, so I would practise in the mornings before school, but when there was a concert or exam looming, she would come to our house at the weekends and make sure that everything was going in the right direction. It would be interesting to know what my mother thought, because she had been a piano teacher herself, and she supervised my practising. As I was always preparing for one or other event, my repertoire was limited over the years, to concertos by Mozart, Mendelssohn and early Beethoven, and showpieces to impress judges and audiences. I missed out entirely on Bach, Mozart or Beethoven sonatas, Chopin or Schubert. It was also unfortunate that Miss Patterson had no imagination and no sense of colour, so it was left to me to try to make the most beautiful sound I could for pieces such as the Nocturne of Grieg and inventing stories to go with the music so that I would have some sense of what the music was about.

When I started studying in London I felt uneducated, but I will always be grateful for the finger technique that I acquired during those early years. There is a complete blank in my memory of why I stopped having lessons with her. Perhaps my mother had painted enough shoes! I suspect it was because, having left school, and having started playing piano trios and doing concerts with other young people, she had lost control and I had reached a point in my pianistic ability when I needed a change.

I never saw Miss Patterson after my last lessons with her. It now seems rather cruel and unfeeling considering that, but for her commitment and knowledge, my life would have been completely different.

Sea And Land

For the first 17 years of my life I lived in sight and sound of the sea. Our home was on the crest of the ridge called the Berea, overlooking the flat land of central Durban. It was actually about five miles from the sea but the sound was always there in the background. This sea, the Indian Ocean, was an intrinsic part of my life. From our balcony I could watch ships arriving and leaving the harbour, especially during the war years, when convoys of ships could be seen anchored in the ocean waiting their turn to dock.

Because this sea was wild, unpredictable, exciting, and dangerous, part of a particular weather phenomenon causing violent seas, I find the tame English seas, and even the ever-blue Mediterranean ocean timid and domesticated.

My ocean was warm, had huge breaking waves, violent undertow, and sharks. It wasn't a place to go swimming, rather a place to challenge the waves to knock you over, or to dive through them under the foaming surf, emerging to meet the next challenge. There was also the challenge of the sharks. They did cause deaths, amputations and fear.

"Always make sure there are people around you," we were told, "never go beyond the other swimmers." But being young and invincible, we forgot what could lay in wait.

All the beaches in South Africa are sandy and Durban had four miles of golden sand. No dunes, no pebbles, just hot, fine sand, which burned my feet and caused me to run on tip toes to the soothing water. We did a primitive form of surfing on our stomachs, riding the waves on boards. Proper surfing hadn't become a sport in those long-ago days.

There were always lifeguards on the beach sitting on built-up high platforms, keeping watch for incidents at sea. They would put up flags, some yards apart, having decided that it was safe to swim in the area between them. From their platform they could watch, not only for swimmers getting into trouble, but for the ominous fins of lurking sharks. When a shark was spotted, just as in the film "Jaws," they would blow a whistle and call everyone out of the water. Of course those tanned, muscular, gorgeous young men attracted a lot of attention from the girls sunning themselves on the golden sand.

The sound of the crashing waves at night permeated my dreams of living below the sea. It was bewitching and colourful there; everything moved with dance-like, dreamy movements. There were mermaids bedecked in floating coloured garments, blue and green, matching the dazzling fish and the waving foliage, and I felt happy and calm and fearless. I think this had the effect of giving me confidence in water and I never had a fear of drowning. Perhaps I really believed that I would be able to breath down there. For years after coming to London I missed the rumbling roll of the waves. I would lie awake at night, listening fruitlessly for that non-existent sound. Some people living in cities, long for the mountains and the lakes, but I always longed to be by the sea.

The environment in which we lived was subtropical. Like the sea, it was untamed, much less civilised than the English landscape which has been my home for so much of my life. The heat and humidity was enervating, although being born into it, it was often debilitating. People would say, "It's not the heat, it's the humidity," but I couldn't differentiate. It was hot. (In fact Durban has an almost constant humidity of 80 degrees.) I never dried myself after my nightly bath. The effort involved would immediately bring me out in a sweat and negate the whole operation. So I waited a few minutes before climbing, wet, into my pyjamas. One boiling night as I looked out of the window, the whole sky and sea was red - on fire.

There were only two seasons: summer, very hot, and winter, just hot. Daylight came at 6am and nightfall at 6pm throughout the year. I got up every morning at 6 in order to practise before it got too hot and before school started at 8, and, as a young child I was asleep by 8pm. I remember being taken to concerts at night, and being desperate to stay awake, but almost always I would find my eyes closing after the interval. It was so embarrassing.

In my mind all the trees were evergreen. That was not true, but the overall picture was lusciously green, and the vivid colour of the flowers and blossoms suited the brilliant light. There were Flamboyant (Flame) trees with brilliant red flowers, and purple Jacaranda. Enormous pine trees stretched into the sky and palm trees lined the streets.

Despite the sunshine and the ease of living, there were disadvantages to living in Durban. One of them, being the cockroaches that inhabited our kitchen, and once I saw a huge spider in the garden, carrying lots of little spiders on its back. Some of the spiders were poisonous, and so it surprised me when I came to England to see people afraid of, what seemed to me, to be tiny, completely innocent creatures.

Bilharzia, a deadly parasitic disease, was present in all the rivers around Durban and we were banned from ever swimming or even paddling in them. This fear was so ingrained that I have never felt happy seeing children swimming and splashing about in the rivers of Europe. Once, when stepping from a rowing boat onto the bank of a river, the boat moved off, and I tumble into the water. My parents didn't seem concerned about me dying of Belhazia, but I worried about it, a lot.

We would sometimes drive down the South coast from Durban to spend an afternoon on the bank or on the river at Amanzimtoti (that is where I tumbled into the water). The drive would be though plantations of sugar cane, high on either side of the car. Occasionally my father would stop and cut a cane for us to suck. I was a terribly anxious child, and, having been brought up never to steal, I was sure that that was what he was doing - stealing. What if he was caught, convicted and imprisoned? I begged him not to do it.

"Don't do it, don't do it. I won't eat it," I yelled futilely from the back of the car.

It ruined the afternoon, which would otherwise have been an idyllic few hours in a tropical paradise.

We could never have picnics sitting on a rug on the grass. Not only were there poisonous spiders and scorpions but, out of the city, in the countryside, there were snakes - green and black mambas, which are amongst the most deadly of all snakes. Fortunately I never saw either of them, except at the Fitzsimons Snake Park on the beachfront. The Green Mamba is about two metres long and emerald green and lives in the trees, sometimes with its upper body hanging from a tree, ready to snap at any potential prey. The Black mamba is even more frightening and deadly. They are Africa's longest venomous snakes, reaching up to 14 feet in length. They are also among the fastest snakes in the world, slithering at speeds of up to 12.5 miles per hour. When cornered, these snakes will raise their heads, sometimes with a third of their body off the ground, open their black mouths, and hiss. If the unfortunate person doesn't run away, the mamba will strike not once, but repeatedly, injecting large amounts of deadly poison with each strike. Before antivenin, a bite was 100 percent fatal, usually within about 20 minutes.

We didn't have lions and tigers in our back yard but there was the occasional monkey, and there were many of them in the green bush just outside the suburbs. They would clamber all over the car and make a grab for any food if a window was left open. I didn't like them

One of the tourist attractions of Durban was the rickshaws. The drivers, Zulu warriors, wore huge feathered headdresses, dangling wild animal skins, wooden and bead ornaments and rattling seed-pods on their white painted legs. They swung along the hot tarmac roads, leaping, and lifting their passengers, whooping and singing. I never got to ride on a rickshaw because my mother's friend thought it was cruel to inflict one's weight on the poor rickshaw driver. Actually she was probably a snob, and wouldn't have been seen dead in such a down-market form of transport. Of course this friend was wrong. They had to earn a living. But her opinion epitomises the split mind-set of the white South Africans (called Europeans). It was quite acceptable for Africans, known as natives (or in anger, bloody kaffirs) to live in shantytowns, to have passes to allow them be out at night, and to be segregated in every possible way. But it would be degrading for the rickshaw boys to pull one of us along. Our servants had to live in small smelly rooms in the gardens of our homes, but it was perfectly all right for them to cook and clean and look after white children.

However, freedom arrived for almost all African workers on Sunday afternoons. The men servants had their hair cut. In our back yard, for instance, the barber would arrive with his instruments, a stool and a cloth to wrap round his victim and, amidst great laughter and singing, smarten up the men, who would then dress in sparkling white shirts, trousers and shoes (this was the only time shoes were worn) and sit on the pavements on either side of the road shouting across at each other. Cato Manor, a mere mile or two away, was the biggest black shanty-settlement in Durban. Newcomers to the city would parade down our street playing homemade guitars (large, empty rectangular tins with only one or two strings attached), and everyone sang. The indigenous harmonies, they always sang in harmony, still thrills me whenever I hear it. Nowadays it is heard universally, and is even used on TV jingles. The unmarried Zulu women who had recently drifted into the city, and were living in Cato Mano, would swagger down our hill; bare breasted with beaded mini skirts, beaded necklaces, and their hair built up with the help of mud and beads into individual hat-like shapes. They were met by wolf whistles and loud banter from the men watching them.

Durban was the most British of the cities in South Africa and people tried to recreate what they imagined life was like "back home". They talked of going "home," they never went, tried to grow English gardens despite the white ants (termites), that would eat, within days, though any piece of wood inserted into the ground, and tried to ignore the climate (besides the heat and humidity, there was 49 inches of rain a year; 23.6 in London), and to wear English clothes.

"Never go out without your gloves already on," my mother told me, putting on her white gloves to go shopping.

South Africa for the white citizens was a colonial paradise. One could live what would seem to people in England, for

107

example, a luxuriously comfortable life without a large income. My parents were far from wealthy, our income coming from a small menswear shop in the city, but we had a detached 3/4 bedroomed house in a lovely neighbourhood, a car (my father always had a car), two servants, and a nanny when my sister and I were small. The money was not easily earned; my father working six days a week in the shop and both my parents spending many a night at home, bent over the dining room table. "Doing the books".

All their friends had at least one or two servants (many people had more), which left the women, in particular, time to spend complaining about the "Servant Problem". I remember eavesdropping on the ladies sewing-meetings and being bewildered. It seemed that the inherent body odour of the African hurt the delicate noses of the bathed and perfumed mistresses. No amount of red Lifebuoy soap and endless encouragement to bathe could reduce this problem. I wonder how distasteful the European odour was to the African nose. There was also the problem of "African Time". All Black Africans have a nonchalant attitude to time and the need for punctuality. They amble about doing the household chores, very sensibly not getting hot and stressed. But it infuriated their faster, more time-conscious employers.

Our servants lived in kayas, separate buildings at the back of the garden. There would be a small room with a bed and a chair and table, and a separate shower room and lavatory. In our garden a hedge of climbing plants screened them from sight. We were severely discouraged from visiting the kayas, but there was a time when our maid brought her newborn baby to stay, and I would sneak out to play with her. We also had a manservant. The person I remember best was called Eylaus and I loved him. He would give us piggyback rides and played games with us. To me he felt like one of the family. One of the other "servant problems" was the fact that these people came from villages, kraals, in the countryside and would annually go back to see their families. Their families were not allowed to live with them in the city, so every year they would have leave to go home. Their absence meant having to find replacements, "clean" them up and teach them to garden, do the house-work or cook.

My mother could somehow teach the boy to cook but she herself never cooked, except for the occasional cake or pudding. She never made the delicious food her mother had created. I think she was trying to put her Russian, Jewish culture behind her.

Occasionally I could escape the African, English and Jewish cultures that surrounded me, by being taken to the Indian Market where I could get a glimpse of the fourth ethnicity that comprised a large part of Durban society. The Indian population of Durban came into being when an English farmer, growing sugarcane in the area, needed a labour force. Because the native Zulus, who had already been confined to reserves, either refused to work or would only work spasmodically, in 1860, indentured labourers from India were brought over. As the industry prospered many more Indians arrived. They were not exactly slaves although their treatment and living conditions were extremely harsh and they had to serve for three or five years before they were given a small amount of money and the option of either being sent home, or staying and buying some land. Many of them stayed, but they were not allowed to live amongst white people. Their homes were on the other side of the ridge where we lived. It was hotter and more humid and mosquitos flourished, but they planted mango, lychee and avocado pear trees and became successful market gardeners.

Over the years, Indians wishing to improve their economic conditions immigrated voluntarily, but life was hard and segregation complete. In 1893, Mahatma Gandhi settled in Durban with his family. Almost immediately he started his life-long struggle for equality and freedom, setting up the Natal Indian Congress to protect the rights of Indians in South Africa but, although it was always passive resistance, he spent many months of his 20-year stay, in and out of prison.

However the market gardening flourished. Initially farmers

used the Grey Street Mosque to trade, but as the number of traders from both Hindu and Muslim backgrounds grew, they moved to the streets. The atmosphere was buzzing, with horse drawn carts and people sitting on the streets attracting potential customers. They had to pay a daily rental fee to Durban town council and because it was unaffordable to travel back and forth from home they were forced to sleep on the pavements or seek shelter at nearby temples. A typical market day started at 4am and ended at 6pm. Farmers reached the market as early as 2am to secure a trading place. There was no access to toilets and there was no protection from extreme weather conditions.

In 1910, the Indian market was built by the city in Victoria Street.

The Victoria Market was the market I had the pleasure of occasionally visiting with my mother. Individual farmers, stood behind their produce, dressed in rather grubby white, long shirts and trousers, often with a white cloth, tied turban-like, round their heads to help with carrying loaded baskets on their heads. The women were in colourful cotton saris, squatting beside their goods which were spread on the ground. There would be a little haggling before delicious tropical fruits would be dropped into a basket and carried to our car by a little black boy. The market also sold fresh fish and live chickens, and multi-coloured spices in jute sacking. Although covered, the market was not enclosed, so that it was relatively cool, and the multitude of smells would waft around without becoming too overwhelming.

The richer Indian traders were not allowed to set up businesses in the main street of Durban, West Street, where my father's shop was, but the street backing onto to it, Grey Street, was entirely Indian. There were little alleyways, narrow lanes and colonnades over the pavements. Shopping there was always an adventure. Exotic whiffs of strange perfumes, and shops overflowing with beautiful fabrics: brilliant red, blue and green shot-silks and chiffons, and desirable gold bangles and rings.

The Indian population of Durban has continued to grow and it is now the largest Indian city outside the subcontinent.

Durban was, and still is, first and foremost, a seaside resort with hotels and apartments lining the road facing the sea. The highlight of the winter season is the July Handicap, a horse-race meeting which takes place on the first Saturday of July at Greyville Racecourse. It started in 1897 and drew punters from all over South Africa. In July Durban is still very warm, not quite as hot as in the summer, so this was the time when holiday-makers, fleeing the colder parts of the country, filled the hotels. It was the best time of the year for my father's business, and I remember him hoping for rain, because that took the visitors off the beach and into the shops.

I never attended an actual race but there was a road though the middle of the course which led from the town centre up to the Berea where we lived, so if there was no race meeting we could drive through and imagine the horses and colourful jockeys galloping round.

The city was growing very quickly during the 1930s/40s but the dominating buildings were still early Edwardian. The City Hall, built in 1910, is an almost exact copy of Belfast's City Hall. That is where the concerts I played in were held, and the building also housed the library. I stopped using the library after I was told off, when returning a book, for scribbling in the margins. I was shocked. I held books in such esteem that I would never have contemplated doing such a thing. I have never felt comfortable borrowing books from libraries ever since. Who knows what I might be accused of?

The Old Station Building was built in 1892. There was much confusion at the time because the architects in London had mistakenly switched the roof plans with those for the station in Toronto, Canada. The Durban roof was capable of supporting more than five meters of snow, but the Toronto station roof collapsed during the first winter!

An important economy of Durban was whaling. The history of whaling in Durban is fascinating and also horrific but it wasn't until 1975 that it was abandoned. I knew little of it at the time but I was once taken by my father to see a huge whale being prepared for "flensing," being cut up and its blubber, flesh and bones separated. The fetid stink was so unbearable that the sight of the giant animal made no impression and I never went near again.

As I knew nothing of the history or the importance of whaling whilst I lived in Durban, I have done some research. Although almost too horrific to contemplate with contemporary eyes, it was very important to the economy and the development of the city.

This is what I have discovered on the web site, "Facts about Durban."

Whaling started in 1907 when the Norwegian Consul in Durban went back to Norway and with a fellow Norwegian, brought two whaling ships back to South Africa. In 1908 they caught and killed 106 huge animals.

The whaling season in Durban lasted from March to September. Because whales migrate northwards past Durban at the start of the Antarctic winter and pass by on their way back south again for summer, the whaling ships could catch many whales without having to travel much more than 150 miles. The whaling ships would sail up close to whales and shoot them with 165-pound metal harpoons loaded with explosive charges. These would explode inside the whale and kill it. The harpoon was attached to the whaling vessel by a rope so that the whale wouldn't sink once it had been harpooned.

The dead whales would then be pumped full of compressed air so that they would float and were towed back to Durban bay and pulled out of the water onto a slipway. From there they were taken to the whaling station where they were cut up (the process called flensing) and their blubber, meat and bone separated. The blubber was rendered down and used to make soap, margarine and cooking fat. Sperm whales were highly valued because the oil was used as lubricants, spermaceti wax used for candles and in cosmetics and pharmaceuticals. Bone and protein meal was used for animal feed and meat extract used to flavour soups. In later years the meat was frozen and became very popular in Japan.

One of the rarest and most expensive products was Ambergris which is actually an intestinal blockage found in a small percentage of sperm whales. Ambergris does not loose its smell for decades and is used in the most expensive perfumes.

Before World War 1 there were 13 whaling companies in Durban but most of them failed so that after the war only 2 companies shared the slipway and the harbour. The smell from the whaling station was so bad and there were so many complaints from near-by residents that the stations were moved further away. The whales were still brought to the harbour, but now they were loaded onto a specially built train, unique in the world. It was specially designed to take one large and two smaller whales. Whaling in Durban was mainly shore based but in 1937 the Union Whaling Company acquired a factory ship called the Uniwaleco which would travel to the Antarctic during the summer and the waters around Madagascar during winter hunting hump-backed whales. There were also smaller vessels known as catchers. They caught and killed the whales and brought them to the factory ship.

There was much less whaling during the war as the Uniwaleco was requisitioned by the navy and was sunk by a torpedo. Many of the newer whaling vessels were used by the South African Navy as minesweepers.

After the war the Union Whaling Company bought another factory ship and trips to the Antarctic were so successful that in 1954, 2200 whales were caught. But the unrestricted whaling resulted in a depletion of the whales and the company was sold to the Japanese five years later.

Durban-based whalers continued to hunt, however and, although experience had made them adept at finding their prey, from 1954 whales were located by plane, and the details of their location radioed back to the whalers. In 1963 a news report stated that the flights began as a ten-day experiment, but proved so effective that aircraft had flown nearly a million miles on whale-spotting missions since 1954. It was recorded that the aircraft had spotted 11,874 whales. Almost half that number were caught and killed by the whalers.

Pressure from conservationists increased and in 1975 whaling was abandoned.

Whale on the bluff in Durban

Waves

Amanzimtoti

Bare breasted

Hair dressing

Victoria Market

City Hall

School

I don't remember learning to read, or can I bring to mind my first lessons with a teacher on the piano. Obviously, my mother being a pianist and a teacher, taught me the piano and I must have picked up reading words, from storybooks read to me as a tiny girl. It is a mystery. But I know I could read when I was very young because I distinctly remember my first day at kindergarten. Was it the first day? Or the first day I remember?

Anyway, I am about four years old, and we are all sitting on the floor with the teacher pointing to the black-board on which she had written words such as "the cat sat on the mat". She is explaining that c sounds kkk and a, aaa and t, ta. I'm completely lost. I know what it says without all of that and I can't make out what she is trying to do. I put up my hand.

"Yes, Anthya," the teacher asks, "what's the matter?"

I tell her that I can read what she has written and she asks me to show her, so I do.

Now that the grownups discover that I can read fluently, I am suddenly a child genius. The result is that no one teaches me to spell, or how to add up. They probably imagine that I will teach myself all that too. It doesn't happen. Someone should have given me some clues: told me which two numbers add up to ten, and some rules about spelling, such as "i before e except after c." I will struggle with these problems for ever.

School proper begins when I am 6. The Durban Girls' College, previously the Durban Ladies' College is a private school about a quarter of a mile away from home. Another thing I wish I had questioned my parents about is the reason why they picked this particular school to send me and my sister to. I assume it was the nearest school to home - about a quarter of a mile away. Marie Stella School, across the road from our school is Catholic, and perhaps one has to be Catholic to attend. Ideally one should be Christian to attend Durban Girls' College, there is a very strict 10% quota for Jewish girls. The result of this is that I am the only Jewish girl in my class. The anti-semitism inherent in the culture is soon to descend on me.

The twice-daily trek from home to school is illustrated beautifully by Shakespeare: "Creeping like snail, unwillingly to school".

I creep twice a day because I go home for lunch, and, although school is only a quarter of a mile away, that's only a measurement on paper. For me the reality is different. It's hot. Leaving my house, walking down the steep hill, turning left, and trudging snail-like up the continuing slope before reaching the plateau and school, then through the gate and down another hill to the back entrance. Going home - walking in the other direction, and then trudging back to school. Too many hills. too little enthusiasm, in fact, no enthusiasm.

And here is yet another question. Why don't I stay at school and have lunch? Most children stay. Is it because at home we are Kosher and the food at school is not? That is a possibility.

To make matters worse the school uniform is totally inappropriate. It was designed to look like the uniform worn at Roedean, an upper-class boarding school in Sussex, England. Someone had decided that this was our sister school. All our clothes are dark bottle green, guaranteed to retain maximum heat. We wear woollen pleated tunics with long black lisle stockings. They are held up by a suspender belt made of an elastic band around the waist with two or three 'slings' attached on each side. The slings end in clips that fit under the stocking and are held in place by a sort of bobble. The bobbles are always breaking off the suspender and getting lost, but I have discovered that an aspirin fits the clip and will do the job just as well. On "gym" days it's easy to slip off the tunic. Under the tunic we wear a white short sleeved, square necked shirt and big, bouffant green bloomers. That's the winter uniform. The summer one is a green cotton dress which is much better, but we still have to wear the tunic twice a week on gym days. There is also a panama hat with a green ribbon and a badge saying, "Nisi Dominus Frustra," our school motto. Some of the walls in the school are painted this dismal green. I make a promise to myself that I will never wear or use that colour as long as I live.

There are about 20 girls in each class and we sit in rows at desks. The desk has a lid, and under the lid is where we keep our books. On top there is an indent for pencils and an inkwell. Once we start using ink there are choices to be made of what sort of nibs suit us best. They all have different names. The important thing is not to make any blots on our work. This is actually very difficult because it all depends on exactly how much ink there is on the nib, and how good the nib is at holding the ink. I used to be quite good at writing with a pencil but sometimes I seem to have no control of the blots.

The thing uppermost in the minds of most South Africans is sport, and despite the ethos of the school to "Transform little girls into young ladies," amongst the pupils, sport is the only thing that counts.

And I can't do it.

I can't play netball because I am afraid of that hard ball winging its way towards my head. I duck.

I can't play tennis. The rule is that before being allowed on a tennis court I first have to bat the ball up and down on the tennis racket innumerable times. The ball falls on the ground.

I can't play hockey. My parents forbid it. The hard ball might damage my precious hands.

Gym. Well, that's altogether impossible. I never succeed in vaulting over the "horse". I run up the spring-board and come to an ignominious halt.

I hang from the rope I am meant to be climbing, my weedy arms unable to pull me up.

I have to lead the class in marches around the gym. I'm the shortest and we line up according to height. I can't understand a word the butch sports mistress is yelling at me in broad Scottish, calling me by the name of the only Jewish girl in the class below me, "Rubens, left march". Blatant anti-Semitism. I can't understand her; I always turn right when she means left or left when she means right. She loves that.

I *can* swim. I can swim quite long distances but I can't

swim quickly so I don't get picked for races. This un-sportiness causes one of the most humiliating experiences I have to suffer. Whenever teams are picked, and there seems to be a lot of that, I am left until last. I understand why this happens, I wouldn't pick me, but because it is repeated virtually every day, I am miserable. I can't persuade my mother to say I am "unwell," (the euphemism for having a period and the excuse for not running around) more than twice a month. It looks suspicious.

My mother and I are also lying about my piano exams. The exams usually take place during school hours, or at least so near to school hours that I have to miss school in order to take them. This is against the rules and I have been refused permission to leave. I am, however, allowed time off to go to the dentist. It is true that I spend a lot of time in the dentist chair, I do have rotten teeth. Despite having to take cod-liver oil and malt and other disgusting substances, my teeth still need a lot of attention. However, not *that* much! So going to the dentist, the lie, enables me to take the exams.

When the good results reach the ears of Miss Middleton, the headmistress, she announces them with pride to the school at the morning assembly. The lie pays off. School teaches me to lie.

This is the school badge and the school motto. It means "Without God all is in vain" and it is the school's principle to have "a strong Christian ethos".

My dictionary says that that means-

showing qualities associated with Christians, especially those of decency, kindness and fairness.

I don't think that the founders of the school, or the head,

or the teachers, have seen my dictionary. For them it seems to mean that anyone who is not an Anglican, or white, is beneath contempt. So the 10% quota of Jewish girls in the school (there are of course, no Blacks, Indians or Coloured girls) can be verbally abused without Christian remorse. I have mentioned our sports mistress but she is not the only one. One day I hand in to my teacher the small piece of embroidery I have been given to do. She picks it up delicately between two fingers, holding it at a distance, and, noticing a spot of blood where I had pricked my finger, says,

"Only a Jew would hand in such a dirty piece of work".

Miss Middleton, our headmistress, has enforced many rules to try to turn her hulking, sporty, girls into "young ladies". The length of our skirts is important. They have to be four inches from the floor when kneeling down. At the beginning of each term we line up on our knees and out comes a ruler. We're taught cooking, embroidery and elocution. Miss Middleton sneers at our South African accents,

"That's not how they speak at Roedean. Diphthongs girls, diphthongs!" What's a diphthong? None of us know.

We are doing Greek Dancing. We wear tunics and are barefooted and do simple walking steps and a number of arm movements which I think are inspired by the American dancer, Isadora Duncan who, in her turn, was inspired by the images on Greek vases and the bas-reliefs in the British Museum. Her dancing was wild and free but ours is so reduced in spirit and so static that all the joy has been removed.

Another of Miss Middleton's rules is that hair had to be short or if long, tied back in a ponytail. It's totally forbidden to have it permed (permanently curling hair is all the rage). So, during Assembly (called prayers), as she stands on the platform behind the lectern, in front of the choir I am not in, she must have noticed that sprinkled amongst the blond tied-back hair there are some curly heads. Strangely enough, most of those belong to Jewish girls. I recognise them from Jewish Assembly. It follows that at least once a term I am summoned to her office and told that I have broken the rule and had my hair permed. No amount of tears from me and letters from my parents telling her that I have naturally curly hair has any impact. She never actually says that only Jews (and Blacks) would have curly hair, but it is implied. Could she be jealous? Her hair is short, straight, and grey.

All this gives the girls freedom to use this overt anti-semitism to bully me. Children will always find the weak point and use it. As well as my uselessness at sports, I play the piano. I don't know any girl at school (except my sister) who plays the piano. I feel isolated. It is possible that there are other girls learning musical instruments, but I am so enclosed in my own misery that I am blind to much of what is going on around me.

Our music teacher, Miss Frost, plays the piano and teaches us singing. This seems to consist of Christian hymns and, as Durban is British through and through, we sing "Rule Britannia," "There'll Always be an England" and "Jerusalem" about building Jerusalem on England's green and pleasant land. England is 6000 miles away, a place of dreams, of stories, of Enid Blyton's Famous Five, and Swallows and Amazons' children sailing their boat on a lake.

When Miss Frost is absent for some reason "they" suddenly remember me, the girl who plays the piano, and I find myself playing hymns and marches for the girls to enter and leave the hall and occasionally I play for Jewish Prayers. (Why don't I go to Jewish Prayers?) It is, however, only on rare occasions that I play the piano; usually I am standing in the hall with a hymn book in my hand, singing hymns and closing my eyes and saying the Lord's Prayer. It still trips off my tongue. I will never forget it.

I am not in the choir. I am truly devastated, it would have made sense, just this once, for me to be chosen. I am always recruited when there is a sight-singing contest because I am probably the only person able to read music and therefore able to sight-sing.

One afternoon my class-room is suddenly empty. I am left alone. I'm so obsessed that I convince myself that everyone has gone off to choir practise, so I pack my bag and leave the school, trudging sadly home. I am half way there when I suddenly realise that choir practice isn't taking place, the girls have gone off to another room for a different lesson. It's too late and too embarrassing to go back, so I continue on my way. The rumpus this causes is amazing. No one knows where I am. I'm not at school and there is no one at home when I arrive. I lie on my bed, my head buried in the pillow. I don't want to face any of this. When my parents return, and the anxiety about my safety calms down, I am left confused and extremely embarrassed and wish to die, or at the very least never, never to go back to school. Never ever, ever.

"Do you want to change schools?" my parents ask "You could go to the Durban High School."

I seriously consider this, but how do I know what I will meet in a new school. I decide it is better the devil I know than one I don't. I could be jumping from the frying pan into the fire. I decide to stick it out and keep my mind on the day I will be leaving. On my return, no one seems to have noticed my absence and schoolwork continues as usual.

England features largely in our history lessons. All history is taught with a right-wing bias and the little South African history we learn is tilted entirely on the side of the brave, white colonialist overcoming the savage black tribes. We learn a list of Kings and Queens of England but we aren't taught anything about the Boer War which was fought between the Afrikaners and the English. We also learn about the Great British Empire. About Robert Clive, who secured India, and the wealth that followed for the British crown, and about James Wolfe, whose victory over the French resulted in the unification of Canada and the American colonies under the British crown. But the Empire was soon to crumble. In 1947 India gains its independence and some of the ruling British (the Raj), who had to leave India, arrive in Durban and continue to behave as if they are still in India: drinking a lot, and calling to their servants, as they sit on their balconies, by clapping their hands. Not a South African habit.

We are taught Afrikaans, which I am good at because of my

holidays in Kimberley where Afrikaans is the spoken language. Here it is taught begrudgingly. No one really needs anything except English in this more than English city, and certainly Zulu, which is the spoken language all around us, is never even considered. We all know a little "Kitchen Zulu," which is all we need to speak to servants.

Geography is better; it has some relevance. We are taught about soil erosion. If the soil is ploughed vertically, that is down the hills and not across, it causes huge crevices to form, called dongas. We are told that the African way is vertical so it was up to the educated English to teach the Zulus the correct method.

Our teacher, Miss Henley, inspires me with her stories of the far-flung countries she had visited (all countries are far flung from South Africa). She shows us some of the souvenirs she has bought, such a sombrero from Mexico or a model of the Houses of Parliament from London. Geography comes alive, and I can't wait to be able to see these places for myself. At the moment the nearest I can get is photographs, and so I persuade my parents to order the National Geographic Magazine, and I start to collect stamps, which teaches me about faraway places and a little of their history.

I enjoy leaning lots of poems from memory in our English lesson. Poems such as "Daffodils" by Wordsworth (I've never seen a daffodil), "Tyger, Tyger Burning Bright" by Blake, and my favourite, "The Listener" by Walter de la Mare, so mysterious and slightly creepy. In Art we learn to draw cubes and circles and other geometric shapes and shade them to give the appearance of roundness or reflection of light. We never have paints or free composition but we learn a simple form of calligraphy which I like. My signature still has traces of that in the A—a rather flamboyant flourish.

I can't see the point of Latin; it's a dead language. Our teacher doesn't enlighten us on how useful some knowledge of Latin could be, and learning by rote the conjugation of verbs and nouns is terribly boring. Translating Roman stories of war into English is even more boring and totally irrelevant.

The only science we do is Botany. This is useful because

it is the nearest we get to sex education. Flowers have female stigmas and male stamens and the stigmas have to be fertilised with pollen from the stamens. It doesn't take much to put two and two together.

Remembering that it is the policy of the school to turn "Little girls into young Ladies", occasionally some celebrated visiting musician is invited to play a short recital for the school. The reaction of the girls is barely suppressed giggles.

A year or so after I had walked through the school gates for the last time, on that day when the sun shone brighter and the huge burden had been lifted from my shoulders, I am invited to return to play a concert after prayers. I am sure the reaction is exactly the same as at every other recital — giggles. But I don't care. They cannot hurt me any more. I am startled and delighted to see that some of the girls who had towered over me have shrunk and I can look down on many of them. I have grown at last. Let them giggle at the music. I don't care. I will never see any of them ever again.

In School Uniform

Third Movement

Development

Growing Up

While Rome Burns - Oil on canvas

Freedom

The day I left school was the day I started to become a musician.

There are "gate-ways" one goes through in life. Sometimes one skips through them with joy and excitement and at other times crawls through, laden with sorrow. And there are times of fear, and of excitement, but my walk out of the gate on the last day of school and through the gate-way to life as a musician, was unique in its relief and its buoyed up feeling of ambition.

I was now fifteen but, up until then, I had hidden my ambition to be a pianist even from myself and certainly from anyone else. I had been a little girl who could play the piano well but if anyone asked, (and adults always asked) what I was going to do when I grew up, I had come up with all sorts of answers. I had seen a film about Madame Curie who was responsible for the discovery of radiation. I would become a scientist and discover the cure for the asthma my mother suffered from. I would be a ballet dancer - imagine! But then I saw the film "A Song to Remember," a fictionalised story of the life of Chopin. A truly terrible film, but it fulfilled all my romantic dreams. Chopin was consumptive and there was a shot of him tearing away at one of his most difficult pieces as the camera moved in to a close-up of the pristine white keys and a circular blob of red blood. How romantic. Somewhere I had heard that most musicians lived and died in poverty, huddled in a garret just like in "La Boheme". Even more romantic. That's what I would do. But all this was fantasy. Walking out of the school gates for the last time was reality, and now I was ready to admit to myself what my real hope and dream was.

My mother warned me of the pitfalls of life as a pianist but, nevertheless, it was quite obvious that she wanted both me and my sister, who was three and a half years younger than me, to fulfill her own thwarted dreams. The mistake here was to have both of us playing the piano. Each of us on a different instrument would have solved many problems. As it was, it created a very competitive atmosphere, and she did nothing to stop this, never really understood it, perhaps even encouraged it. We both had to practise before school every morning and there were two wonderful pianos in the houses to choose from. Somehow, for no reason that I can now imagine, one of them would become the favourite for both of us and we would fight for it.

I mean really fight: proper physical fights, punches, kicks, bites. Lorraine was short enough to jab me in the shoulders with her very pointy chin. It hurt a lot. I remember throwing a piano stool to the ground and breaking its legs off rather than letting her have it. Both pianos were equally good. Why did no-one stop this?

But now I had left school there was no need for the early morning fights. Lorraine could have any piano she wanted, I would have all day after she had left, to practise in peace.

My mother, Gertie, always supervised my practice, usually just listening in from a different room and poking her head round the door with unwanted advice. She was making sure that I was learning the piece I had been given, not messing about, not finding lovely chords, not improvising by ear. However, I did discover a wonderful cheat. I could play scales and read a book at the same time. The book was hidden by an open piece of music, which is what my mother saw from the door, and I could rush up and down the piano in every major of minor key, arpeggio or broken chord, whist continuing to read. I became very, very good at scales, and can still knock them off at speed whenever I need to show what fun they can be to a reluctant pupil.

I felt hurt and upset that my mother never expressed, either in words or actions, the pride or joy she surely must have felt at my achievements. Perhaps she was afraid of spoiling me, making me big-headed. She was not a cold person, but until her grandchildren came along, she was unable to be tactile, to hug or kiss. She was a very beautiful woman, aware of her beauty, and had hoped and perhaps expected me to follow in her footsteps. I never thought that I lived up to her expectations. There was always something wrong. My nose was too wide.

"Keep pinching it," she advised. My lips were also too wide.

It was the fashion to have thin lips, always painted red.

"Keep biting your lips together," she told me.

I was certainly too fat. Always too fat. Even as an adult she would tell me of Mrs... who had just lost two stone on the "what ever" diet. It was not a direct hit but I always knew what she meant.

The result of this criticism was that I never had any confidence in my appearance, and never believed anyone who said I looked lovely.

On my 15th birthday my poor mother made another attempt to mould me into the sociable, friendly girl I should have been, and decided to make a party for me. I was horrified. Who would she ask? I hadn't made any friends at school. I was a misfit. Jewish and a pianist. I didn't know how to relate or what to talk about. So she had invited the children of her friends, whom I knew, but they were not my friends. Having arranged this, she took me out to buy some shoes with highish heels, a suitable party dress, and spent some time showing me how to make up my face. I have blocked the party out of my memory but I do remember preparing for it, sitting in front of a mirror, trying to put on lipstick, and crying.

So although stepping into my new life was a challenge that I couldn't wait to undertake, I was still very self-conscious, shy and really a loner. Things had to change.

The first change was that we all went on holiday, our very first family holiday. Before that, the war and the need to earn a living had kept my parents busy. We went by car, first to Brakpan to see Auntie Frieda and the family, and then on to Kimberley to visit my grandparents. From there we set off for Cape Town. That part of the journey was new to me. We drove for hundreds of miles through the Karoo on long, arrow-straight deserted roads, surrounded by the dry, scorching semi desert. The sky above was pure blue, not a cloud to be seen.

I had no idea at the time, that the indigenous San people (Bushmen) had lived in this area before they had been wiped out by the white man's small-pox and measles, and by the farmers who had fenced off their properties, leaving the hunter gatherer San, nowhere to wander. They had left behind wonderful rock paintings and carvings, but in 1948 little was known of these amazing art works, so we didn't stop to explore but continued though the repetitive, seemingly lifeless landscape. It was hypnotic, like sailing in a ship on a sea of sand.

As we neared the ocean the landscape changed, it became hilly and green and full of grape vines. And then we were in Cape Town. It was even more spectacular than all the picture postcards I had seen. We went up Table Mountain in a cable car and watched the land and sea below disappear as we swung up though the famous cloud which often shrouds the mountain. From down below it looks like, and is often called, "The Tablecloth".

We drove down to the most southerly point of Africa where the warm Indian Ocean bumps into the cold Atlantic, passing though vegetation unique to that area, known as fynbos (evergreen shrub-like plants with fascinating flowers). Large troops of baboons, also indigenous to that part, threatened anyone who dared to get out of their car.

Whilst in Cape Town I met, for the first time, my father's youngest brother Lawrence, always called Lorry. A tall, glamorous man, known in the family as a lady's man. Our stay with him was very short, so it was not until many years later, when my husband Raymond and I stayed with him whilst on a concert tour around the Cape, that I had the great pleasure of finding out how much like my father Lorry was in his kindness and generosity. Leaving Cape Town we headed east on the way home, a thousand miles away.

But first we stayed with Issie's sister Gertie, who was married to another Uncle Solly. They owned and ran a hotel in the seaside town of Strand, only 30 miles from Cape Town. Auntie Gertie was small and plump, the very antithesis of my mother Gertie. I think my father was very fond of his sister and I felt sorry for him because they had so little contact, so few meetings, so many hundreds of miles apart. I hope they wrote to each other, but somehow I doubt it. Issie didn't write. In the two years I was in

England whilst he was still in Durban, I never once had a letter from him. Sometimes there were a few words at the bottom of the twice-weekly letters from my mother. As I never expected more, it was fine by me.

We drove home through the Garden Route, a stretch of the Eastern Cape coastline of spectacular natural beauty with sandy beaches, lakes, lagoons, mountain passes and one of the mildest climates in the world. It was the Garden of Eden. I was to discover very soon how this Eden, and indeed the whole of South Africa, was being ruined by mad politics - the Snake in the Garden.

As I was only fifteen, it was my parents' view, and mine too, that I needed to be educated. They had arranged for me to have a tutor and they had brilliantly found the perfect person to fill that role. His name was Lex Levine and I was to go to his house two afternoons a week.

I took the tram for the short ride to his house. As I stood at the stop, on the main road at the bottom of our hill, I could see tracks on the tarmac that I was sure could only have been made by a runaway tram (one of the double decker electric trams, running on rails and attached to electric cables above). I could visualise one of them becoming derailed, toppling over, or worse still, running straight into me standing at the stop. I never told my parents of these anxieties. I could just imagine them saying, "You're over imaginative. Stop reading all those books." But perhaps in the end, this imaginative trait was necessary for my development as a musician.

However, I always arrived at Mr. Levine safe and sound, and was shown into his study by his wife. He was usually bent over some papers but cleared them all away on my arrival so that we would have some space for my lesson. I knew that he was the principal of the Durban Indian College, in itself a unique position for a redheaded white Jew, but other than that, I knew nothing about him and was much too shy to ask personal questions.

His study was a small room at the front of his house. Rather dark and cool, sheltered from the heat by the leaves of a "Flamboyant" tree which was covered in brilliant red blossom in summer-time. The walls of the room were lined with books. How I wished we had a room like that in our house. Both of us sat facing the window at one side of a large wooden desk. If the lessons had not been so fascinating, I could have lost myself in the beauty of the tree.

My mother had given him a list of subjects I was to study including Latin, I remember, because although her ambition for me was to become the greatest, most famous pianist in the world, perhaps only second to my sister, I had also to be prepared for the possibility that I would become a doctor. In order to become a doctor, Latin was a necessity. The whole thing was little insane. Mr. Levine soon found out that I hated Latin and it only lasted a week or two. His idea was for me to concentrate on Shakespeare. It was a stroke of genius.

We read the plays, not only for the drama, or even really for the poetry, but for the understanding of the words and their meaning, and to delve into the history and the politics.

I was privileged to have this highly educated and sensitive man teaching me. The wonderful thing for me, sitting in Mr. Levine's study, was that I believed he was treating me like a university student at a tutorial, and I loved it. He quickly and painfully made me aware of the situation in which I was living: how easy it was to take for granted the social system which decreed that people with different skin colour had to be separated and forced to live totally disparate lives. An Indian college existed because Indian students could not go to a White college, and Mr. Levine was there because it was assumed that no Indian would be suitable (educated enough) for that position.

Our afternoons together would go something like this.

We could be reading Richard 2nd. He would stop. "Do you know what infidel means?" Out would come his enormous dictionary. "It means someone of a different religion (it could equally be colour), and its origin is Latin "fides"-faith or "fidere" to trust."

So then a political and philosophical discussion would

ensue. I learned what was going on, how political events could be manipulated, and how to recognize propaganda. It was a revelation, an education. But it was also unsettling. The people living around me seemed blind. How was it possible for them to trust their black servants utterly, but to be so seemingly unaware, but also frightened, of the faceless millions who were being pushed further and further into racial segregation.

My parents never uttered a derogatory word against the native people, but it certainly was common to hear people ranting on: "The black man is just a monkey completely incapable of being educated." They were the work force but because there were so many of them: "We have to keep then under control," they said. So they lived in shantytowns with no sewerage and no electricity. Restricted and segregated.

No Blacks on a bench. No Blacks on the grass. No Blacks on White buses. No Blacks in cinemas. No Blacks in "European" shops, not even as assistants, only as cleaners. Blacks must carry permits at all times or else be jailed. (My father often had to go to the police station to bail out our servant). It was amazing that we could lead such seemingly untroubled lives. Mr. Levine was sure that it could not last.

Because my parents were not great readers, and at that time there were no newspapers, magazines or radio programmes discussing books, I was completely lost as to what to read. Once Mr. Levine discovered that I was a voracious reader, it became another topic of exploration. He gave me a book list and lent me his own books, which broadened my interests and my education. There have been some extraordinarily lucky circumstances in my life and being taught by Lex Levine is one of them.

He was my hero.

Me at 15yrs old

Road in the Karoo

Europeans only.

No Blacks on the Beach

Moving On

My parents have been working away behind my back, not only finding Lex Levine, and Moira Birks who is going to be teaching me the piano, but also Roy Carter who will be my cello teacher. I am of course, not going to be a professional cellist, but I love the sound of the instrument and it will broaden my horizons and be a lot of fun. My father has come home with a cello, (goodness knows where he found it), but has completely forgotten about a bow. A little while later he arrives in a state of shock with a bow. He has had to pay £5 for it. "Just a stick with some horse hair!" he stormed.

My piano lessons with Moira Birks are a disappointment. She is at the height of her career as a concert pianist, has a formidable technique, and looks very cool and very pretty on stage. She is playing all over South Africa as well as bringing up her four children. Her husband is a singer, and I think she has to be the main breadwinner, so at this point in her life, teaching is not her main preoccupation and she keeps me at arm's length. I believe that in later years when she was concentrating more on teaching, she was able to delve deeply into the music, explaining about structure and phrasing, but I miss out on that. I am just given the next piece to play and the rest is left to me. As time goes on, I am invited to do quite a lot of concerts and broadcasts and, as a performer herself, she understands which pieces of music are most suitable and her critiques of my performances are helpful. However, I feel sure that I need more, and so will have to move on sometime soon.

But then there is Roy Carter, the principle cellist of the Durban Municipal Orchestra, the orchestra I have played piano concertos with. He is charming, warm and enthusiastic and is making learning fun. My mother is bowled over by Roy. He is the first charismatic musician she has met and she is smitten. Although not classically good looking, he has the sex appeal that draws even the most incorruptible woman to him. My sister and I suspect that our mother is having an affair with him. She talks about him at every opportunity and pops into my lessons to ask unnecessary questions about my progress. If she is serious about any sort of liaison with Roy, she will have to get past Roy's wife Valerie, who knows her husband and keeps a very wary eye on him, keeping as close as possible to him at all times. She is not stupid.

Although I am aware of his charm, he certainly doesn't want a droopy adolescent making his life difficult, and in any case, I am not conscious of the sexual attraction. I just like him very much. He has his own teen-age children to cope with. Peter John, later known only as Peter, is a very talented young violinist and Glory, is studying the piano.

Glory doesn't want to be a pianist and although we occasionally play duets together, it is clear that she is doing it under duress. My sister and I have tried playing duets, but it is useless. You have to really get on with a duet partner - sitting up close, crossing hands. It's better if you're lovers doing it for fun. But even then there will be rows about who plays the treble part, who the bass, who turns the pages, who uses the pedal. Lorraine and I just fight.

Despite Valerie's wary eye (perhaps because of it), the Carter and Israel families become friends. Even though the cello is never going to be my first instrument, it has opened many doors to me. Piano playing is very isolating. You sit in a room on your own obsessively going over and over a difficult passage and, even when you finally achieve something you are satisfied with, you only please yourself. You are only going to perform it on your own. The piano is complete in itself. Even when you play a concerto with orchestra, the piano is a giant instrument in front of the orchestra - not a part of it. It is only after you have gained a great deal more experience, and are lucky enough to play chamber music (with other instruments) that you all become one whole.

When you start learning a string or wind instrument you come quite quickly into contact with other players. Because you are not complete on your own, you will need someone to accompany you and you could soon start playing in an orchestra - a children's orchestra perhaps. You will sit next to someone else, share the music stand, and listen to all the sounds around you. You are only a part of something bigger and better than yourself. Of course, as you progress, you too will have to spend hours in a room on your own obsessively going over and over a difficult passage. The world outside fades into insignificance. That's why people think musicians are mad!

"He's just a mad musician," they say. Perhaps they are right.

I am finding learning the cello easier than I had first imagined because I have come to it knowing all the basic rules of music. I don't have to learn to read or to count, as absolute beginners have to do. What I have to do is to find out the exact angle and height the cello has to be between my legs, where to put my fingers, how to hold the bow and how to move it across the strings. I don't suppose I am making a very beautiful sound, but I am playing, and am finding reading really easy. I struggle with sight-reading on the piano. There is always so much to read, so many notes, two staves vertically apart with different notation, lots of chords which could, at worst, use all ten fingers. But on the cello there is just one line, virtually no chords. Sight-reading is suddenly easy. Well, anyway, at this beginner's level, it is easy.

I progress quickly enough to find myself playing in an orchestra for Gilbert and Sullivan's "Trial by Jury" at a school. I am terrified at first, it is like being thrown into the deep end of a pool of sound. Besides, I don't know any one there and I don't even like the music, but it's not a complicated part, and after the first few rehearsals, I begin to relax and enjoy myself. When I can tear my eyes from the music and look at the stage, everyone there is having fun and the audience is loving it.

Roy Carter's best friend, the violinist Sterling Robbins (Robbie to us all), is the leader of the Municipal Orchestra and he conducts an amateur/student orchestra, the grandly named Durban Philharmonic Orchestra. Having broken the ice with Gilbert and Sullivan, Roy persuades me to join Robbie's orchestra. I have been to many orchestral concerts, but the experience of sitting right in the middle of the sound is overwhelming. Robbie is very ambitious for his orchestra, even giving us some Wagner to play. "Wagner!"

Here now, I am not sitting alone with my piano, I am surrounded by people who have a joint aim, to produce a beautiful, powerful piece of music. At last I have found a place where I feel comfortable. No one cares about my lack of sporting prowess or what religion I practise and we have shared experiences to talk about.

But I still have problems. I am in the throes of growing up and am very emotional about things at home and the relationships in my family. I find the bickering and arguments between my parents very disturbing and upsetting. It seems to me that Gertie endlessly finds something to get agitated about and I feel so hurt for my father that one day I write a note and leave it on his pillow.

"How and why do you put up with her?"

Afterwards I am really ashamed of this, but no one ever mentions it. It might never have happened, and the bickering goes on. I am beginning to wonder if they are even aware that they are doing it.

I fight for more independence and argue with my mother about the style of clothes I want to wear. I design a dress I would like our dressmaker to create, and despair, because my mother is convinced it will make me look fat. I win that argument. She was wrong. For once I'm actually quite pleased with how I look. And, I'm worrying about boys. All the boys I have met so far are either too young or too old for me - or so I think. It's probably an excuse, because in fact I am too shy, too young and too innocent to know how to behave. I decide to write about my problems in a diary so that when I have teen-age children of my own I can read it and remember.

When I start playing in the Philharmonic Orchestra I make my first best friend. Margaret, a violinist (a pupil of Robbie), is a little older than me and she has a car. She picks me up from home and drives me to the City Hall where the orchestra rehearsals take place. My parents only allow me to go with

Margaret if she promises to park the car just outside the Artist's Entrance. This is usually difficult because we are not the only people parking there and, quite honestly, we don't try too hard. We don't see the danger, but for my parents, the image of two young white girls walking even a hundred yards or so on the street at night, scares them.

After the rehearsal when we get back to my house, we sit in the car and have proper intimate conversations. We gossip about the people in the orchestra, talk about the music, about our future plans and complain a lot about our parents.

"They overprotect us. They would be furious if they knew we were sitting in the dark, late at night, open to attack".

There is such an inbuilt fear of the native man that the fact that it is illegal for black men to roam the streets at night does not alleviate their anxiety. The curfew works and the streets are deserted. All parents fear for their children, but we know we are invulnerable and think they are just being ridiculous.

This over-protectiveness also drives me mad when it disrupts the friendship I am building with Jenny, the girl who lives down the road, less than a hundred yards away. Somehow I have discovered that she too is an avid reader, and I love having someone to talk to about favourite characters and stories, and someone to swap books with. She is still at school so I visit her in the evenings. To my extreme annoyance I have to tell my parents what time I am coming home so that they can send someone to escort me.

"It's just across the road", I shout.

"Otherwise you can't go at all".

"But I go there by myself".

"Not after dark. You can't be on the street after dark".

"It's only 7 o'clock".

I can't win the argument and do want to see Jenny, so I succumb.

The reality is that since this is the beginning of the Apartheid era, the Nationalist Government having just won the election, there is simmering unrest all over South Africa. In the location of

Cato Manor, just about a mile away from where we live, there are about 30,000 Zulu squatters living on land which belonged, until they arrived, to Indian Market Gardeners. Many of them came during World War 2 because of Durban's booming economy and in 1948 riots break out between the Indians and the Zulus, spreading over parts of the city and killing over 100 people. No wonder my parents are anxious.

The incredible thing is that in a year or two they will leave me in London on my own and, at that time, they don't warn me about the dangers of being out at night, or about anything else as it happens. London doesn't have black men so is perfectly safe. Little do they know.

Roy Carter has another ground-breaking scheme afoot.

I will be the pianist in piano-trios concerts with his son Peter and one of his more advanced cello pupils. I have never before played any chamber music. Never, if truth be told, even heard any. I think that, as a cellist, he ignores the fact that in most chamber music involving a piano, the pianist has by far the most difficult, not to say dominating, part to play. So he hands me the Mendelssohn D minor trio and the Schubert B flat trio and says,

"Learn the first movements of both of these. I think that will do for the moment."

When I get home and look at the Mendelssohn, I'm aghast. There are millions of notes and it goes really, really fast. I have played some Mendelssohn before and I think that, with a lot of work, I may be able to manage it, but the Schubert is a whole new world for me. It's one of the most beautiful pieces of music ever written and really needs maturity to fully understand it. (Many years later these two trios will feature frequently in the repertoire I play professionally.) After a week or two of frantic practicing, Mr. Carter arranges a rehearsal for the three of us, which he supervises. It is just as well because I think he is being very ambitious for us, we are very young and this is new to all of us. After a while he achieves a result he is happy with and organises some concerts.

Ruth Bennet is the cellist. She will spend much of her adult professional life as a cellist in the Northern Symphonia Orchestra in Newcastle (England), but now, she is very quiet and even shyer than me. Peter Carter is about a year younger than me and is still at school. As an adult, living in London, he will become world renowned as the leader of the Allegri String Quartet. As it happens, both of us will spend most of our adult life playing chamber music, so this was the perfect beginning.

We play in church halls, school halls, nowhere very important, but it is such good experience and it's fun playing with other people. I am slowly learning that the most difficult, but the most important thing about playing with other instruments, is having to listen to them as well as to myself so that we will always be together in time and dynamic. Also it is most important that the piano should never be too loud and drown out the other instruments.

We have quite long car journeys from home and back to these venues and I decide that I will have to find out something about cricket because that is Peter's main topic of conversation. So I ask my father to explain something about the basics. The details remain a mystery, and I pretend to be more knowledgeable than I am.

Peter has homework to do so he spends the intervals of the concerts catching up with schoolwork. Not having a brother, I had no idea of the naughtiness boys could get up to, so his essay on a "Family Argument" delights me but also on one level shocks. It goes like this:

"No I didn't"

"Yes you did"

"No I didn't "

"Yes you did"

For pages and pages. The length required for the essay.

"You're not going to hand that in," I say.

He, being Peter, does.

He doesn't get expelled. I think it's brilliant.

Friendship with the Carters has put my parents in touch with other players in the orchestra and thus nearer to the performers who are now, since the ending of the war, beginning to arrive from all over Europe. Some of them come to play in the orchestra, to settle in a safe haven having suffered terribly in the concentration camps, both from the Germans and the Japanese.

Stephan Deák is especially memorable. He is a Hungarian violinist, who, so I was told, had recently been released from Dachau and is now in Durban to play solos and join the orchestra. He's a wonderful player, full of gypsy temperament, but the torture he suffered having his fingernails pulled out one by one, catches up with him and he has a complete breakdown, running down the streets naked and screaming - a real shock for the suburban ladies, and so painful for those of us who know him. When he recovers, after spending some time in hospital, he decides never to play the violin again, never to be the focus of attention as a soloist. So now he plays the viola where he can sit quietly in an orchestra, and that is what he did for rest of his life, even when later he lived in London and was a member of the Philharmonia Orchestra.

Of course we didn't know everyone who played in the Durban orchestra and, sadly, one person we didn't get to know, was a violinist called Joe Cowan. Many years later, when I was married to Raymond Cohen and asking him about his family, his father's brothers and sisters, he mentioned that he had an uncle who was a violinist who had gone out to South Africa.

"Did he continue playing?" I asked

"Oh yes."

"Where?"

"Oh my God! I think it was in Durban."

What a coincidence. Why didn't my parents know him? They had friends who were orchestral members, and definitely knew most of the Jewish population. Well, it turned out that he had changed his name from Cohen to Cowan and married a non-Jewish woman. We made some enquiries and found out that Joe and his wife had died but that he had a daughter who was still in Durban. Unfortunately, by the time Raymond and I went out there to do a concert tour, she too had died but we met and became friendly with her husband.

Not only are musicians arriving to settle in Durban, but numbers of celebrity performers such as the violinist Yehudi Menuhin the pianist Claudio Arrau and are coming to give concerts or play concertos with the orchestra. We go to hear them all, and I often pluck up the courage to go back-stage and get autographs. There are even occasions when a star pianist comes to our house to practise on our piano before a concert.

One of the problems my parents had been worrying about behind my back is now being openly discussed. What am I to do and where am I to go with my music from here? I have outgrown studying the piano in Durban, but what to do next? My brave mother, the one I had spent so much time and effort complaining about, decides that, if it is possible, she will try to get help not only from the "foreign" musicians now living in Durban, but also from the visiting celebrities. Of course, without hearing me play they will probably think she is a stage mother pushing her miserable daughter. At this time Shirley Temple, the curly haired, singing and dancing child star is inspiring mothers to groom their little girls to be the next star. I personally know a girl who has actually been taken off to Hollywood to try her luck. She is soon back in Durban.

Gertie does manage to arrange for me to play to a number of visiting musicians. They come from different parts of the world, and fortunately for both my mother and me, they agree that I am talented enough and should go on studying. Unfortunately they all insist that I go to study in which ever country they come from, so the whole thing is still a muddle.

Talking it through, we decide that I have to be somewhere where English is spoken, so that would be either America or England. America is too far away and too unknown, whereas I had England instilled into me all those years at school. I should feel at home there. I have consistently been awarded very high marks and an annual bursary in my Associated Board music exams, and due to that, have been offered a scholarship to the Royal Academy of Music in London. That would have been the perfect solution except for the fact that all the English musicians we have spoken to warn us off it,

"You will waste an enormous amount of time there and, at the moment, the teaching is not outstanding."

So the search is on for a private piano teacher in London.

One day, after answering the phone, my mother hands it to me.

"It's for you," she says, looking as surprised as I feel.

"H- h- hello " I stammer.

"Hello," came the answer in a very foreign male voice. "My name is Mr Gerodi and I am ringing to ask if you would like to come and play some trios with my wife and me. We heard you playing on the radio, and we were at one of your trio concerts. We loved your playing and would be delighted if you could come." It turns out that he is Hungarian, hence the flattery and the charm.

I continued to stutter.

"W-what do you play?" I ask.

"I am a cellist and my wife is a violinist. Of course we only do this for fun. I am really a scientist."

I have no option but to agree, so he gives me their address and we arrange a time. It is a revelation. I had no idea that people played chamber music for fun. Mr. and Mrs. Gerodi are middle Europeans with all the culture and learning that comes with that. They had escaped from Hungary just before Hitler exterminated virtually all the Jews of Hungary, and had lived and worked in London until his job moved to Durban. I think they are as pleased to have found me as I am to have found them. Like Mr. Levine's house, theirs too is full of books, but they also have beautiful Hungarian embroideries and dark, mysterious paintings, and when I eat with them, it is spicy goulash and poppy-seed pastries. Very exotic.

The whole family become friendly and the Gerodis are very keen to offer advise on my further studies. They know the music scene in London, and like all good Hungarians, know all the best Hungarian musicians living there.

"You must have lessons with our friend Illona Kabos," they tell me, and so Illona Kabos goes down on the list of people I will need to do auditions for when, and if, I go to London.

As the weeks go by, it seems more and more obvious that I will definitely be going for two or three years to "continue my studies". I am so busy doing my own thing that it comes as a surprise to discover that a passage on a ship has been booked and that the whole family will be travelling to London. My father has an insurance policy which has matured and they are going to use this as an opportunity to visit as much of Britain as possible and then, on a Cook's tour, to see as much of Europe as they can.

So what was I feeling about all this? Why was I not feeling really frightened and nervous about leaving behind everything and everyone I know? Somehow it seemed that my life so far had been leading up to this, and that this was just the next gateway I had to step through.

I had been inspired to travel by my geography teacher at school, and the thought of everything London could offer, excited me, and I was at the age when freedom from parental rules and protectiveness was very tempting. I was longing to do whatever I pleased.

I did look back on incidents in my "career" as a pianist thus far, remembered the very first concerto I had played aged nine and my feelings which afterwards I expressed to my father,

"All that work, and it was over in 15 minutes."

Then there was the frightening experience, when I was a little older (about twelve), of suddenly waking up as if from a dream and finding myself on stage playing with an orchestra in front of hundreds of people. Up until then performing had just been one of those things I did, like going to school, or for a swim, but at that moment, in the middle of a performance, it was very frightening. Somehow, I don't know how, I went on playing, didn't even stumble, but never again would I be able to perform completely nerve free.

There was the wonderful experience of playing chamber music and the fun I had had learning the cello. I was taking my cello with me and I hoped I would be able to continue with that.

Over the years I had become a performing musician, and I wanted to continue. I would have to see where the next few years led me.

Peter John, me and Ruth Bennet

Voyage

We're off

Before I set forth on the big adventure, I would have to say goodbye to my grandparents and my aunts and uncles. Fortunately my cousin Milton's Barmitzvah fell just at the right moment, as it was an occasion when everyone would be together in Kimberley - it was perfect.

As I fully expected to be returning within two or three years, saying goodbye was not a sad occasion, but it must have been strange for my grandparents to be seeing me off back to Europe, from whence they had fled fifty years before. They all promised me presents. My Uncle Joe had arranged for the Readers Digest to be regularly delivered to me. (I didn't have the heart to tell him that I had outgrown it years before). My Aunty Frieda's huge tin of Quality Street sweets however, was much appreciated.

My parents and sister rushed straight back to Durban. They had all the packing and arrangements to be made for our epic journey, leaving me behind for more time with the rest of the family; time for longer farewells. All the Kimberley relatives came to see me off when Aunties Frieda and Ida drove me to Johannesburg airport. I flew back to Durban on my own.

This was both exciting and frightening. Flying was not at all common then and I remember after taking off, the plane banked steeply (as is often the case) and I really thought, as I saw the ground looming up outside the window, that my last day had come. It took many years and many flights for me to overcome my fear of flying.

We set off on the four-week voyage to England in June 1950 a few days after my 17th birthday. The ship on which we were making this momentous journey was a small cargo vessel, the "Umgeni", not one of the luxury liners, (the Union Castle Line) that regularly plied the Atlantic between England and South Africa. That would have been much too expensive. This was really basic: my sister Lorraine and I sharing a cabin with four other women: very small, like a couchette on a French overnight train; there was hardly room to turn around. I don't remember who the other four women were, as I spent as little time as possible in there. Fresh water to drink and to wash one's face and hair was available in the toilet along the passage, otherwise, for every other purpose, there was only salt water from the sea. Warm, salty, dirty looking water. Ugh!

The first week was spent going from one South African port to another picking up cargo and a few passengers. My parents really loved this, because we could disembark in each town and visit one of my mother's numerous relatives. The best part for me was having a bath in their elegant bathrooms, using their fresh hot water. We sailed into Cape Town on a clear and sunny day, much colder than Durban where it never got cold. It was the middle of winter and a harbinger of what a cold winter day might be like in London. We had sailed out of Durban with its rather violent sea, and had had a taste of what it was going to be like leaving Cape Town: quite rough. The sea round the south of Africa and heading north has always been one of the world's most dangerous coastal stretches. In 1497, the Portuguese explorer, Bartolomeu Diaz was the first to sail so far south. He named it the "Cape of Storms," but didn't land, just turned his ship back to safety. Later, in order to tempt more explorers to find the sea route to the east, it was renamed the "Cape of Good Hope," but it took another one hundred and fifty years for the Cape to be settled, this time, by the Dutch East India Company. They set it up as a trading post, somewhere to restock their ships on the way to the East.

"Cape of Storms" was the more appropriate name because so many ships had been wrecked. The coast is littered with their skeletons. These dangerous seas engendered many legends, the most famous of which, is the story of a phantom ship, "The Flying Dutchman", manned by the ghosts of men who had committed terrible crimes and were doomed to sail in these waters forever. Richard Wagner wrote his opera the "The Flying Dutchman" using that story.

We left Cape Town in blazing sunshine, but that didn't last long. We were almost immediately into one of the legendary storms. Dark purple clouds, whipping rain, and violent winds buffeted the little ship. It seemed that my father and I were the only people not suffering from severe seasickness, everyone else had retired to bed.

"Let's go on deck," my Dad said, "I'm going to see if I can get this on film."

I had always loved the sea and was not afraid. It was exciting: waves breaking over the deck and the ship plunging and lurching in all directions. By the next morning all was calm, and now we had three weeks ahead of us with no obligations and nothing to do. This was going to be unutterably boring.

I was mistaken. My parents went into action. Issie organised deck games: quoits, shuffleboard, ten-pin bowling using anything he could get hold of. And my mother? Well, of course there was a piano on board. An old upright piano. I'm convinced that if there hadn't been a piano, we would not have been on that ship. I sometimes wonder if she shipped it herself so that I could practise. After all, I would have to be playing to prospective teachers almost as soon as we landed. But that was not all. Gertie auditioned everyone on board including the officers, to see what hidden talents they had. There seemed to be a lot, so she arranged shows, and sing-songs, and played the piano for them. Needless to say, her talented daughters performed their party pieces. The evenings were full of music and jokey monologues.

I loved being on the ship at sea, on deck, staring out at nothing but blue, and now heading north towards the equator, the weather was becoming warmer and warmer. I was also being pursued by one of the young English officers. He wasn't the most good looking of the sailors, but this was the first time that any man had flirted with me and it was very exciting, especially when he asked if he could kiss me. How polite. Of course I agreed and that was my first proper kiss. He was officially forbidden to make friends with the passengers, but the poor chap was starved of female company and I was one of the few accessible young women on board. It obviously couldn't go any further, I would have been appalled if he had even suggested it, and in any case I was sharing a cabin with five other people.

When we were within a day's voyage of the equator the crew became very busy organising the ritual of "Crossing the Line". I have read that it was originally some sort of initiation ceremony for sailors who were crossing the equator for the first time. Apparently King Neptune informs the Captain that he will be coming aboard, and that all the novices will undergo some sort of humiliation. Usually, this is performed by the crew, but on the "Umgeni" it was carried out by the passengers. First of all an impromptu swimming pool was rigged up and costumes were improvised out of ship's roping. It turned out to be a hilarious performance. My father, Issie, was dressed up as Neptune with a very ill-fitting wig of long strands of rope which constantly slipped and fell off, and as his throne was set on the edge of the swimming pool, the wig had to be rescued dripping wet from the water. So he held onto it with one hand, whilst carrying the trident, (a three pronged fork on a long stick) in the other. Balancing on his throne proved hazardous and he played up the joke in his best comedian manqué style, constantly falling into the water. One by one various young children, including my sister, were thrown into the pool as a metaphor for the humiliation of the uninitiated, and in the end everyone concerned was in the water, having a whale of a time. The result of all of this was that the pool was left on board and regularly filled with seawater. At last, somewhere to cool off.

Now we were heading for the Canary Islands and a game ensued. Who could be the first to spot land? We were to call out, "Land Ahoy," and rush to tell the Captain. And there it was, the island of Los Palmas, the first land we had seen for two weeks. Frustratingly, the ship didn't dock. It just dropped anchor and the passengers stared at beautiful green trees.

However, within minutes there was a flotilla of little boats with all sorts of tempting things to buy, bobbing up and down within reach of the lowest decks. A lot of young boys were standing on the boats begging us to throw money to them so that they could dive down to the seabed to retrieve the coins. Older men in the boats stood and held up beautiful linens. Madeira, one of the neighbouring Canary Islands, is famous for its hand embroidered linen tablecloths, and these were eagerly bought by the women on board, my mother amongst them. The money and goods were handled by the crew, from the lowest deck. Even after the ship had weighed anchor and set sail away from Los Palmas, the little boats tried to keep up, waving tablecloths in the air.

Suddenly there was only one more week to go before we would arrive in Hull. The time now started to rush away. I worried that if I really hated it in London, whether I would be able to face the humiliation of retreating back to Durban. I didn't think I could, and so made up my mind to put that thought aside, and start practising with more enthusiasm.

Crossing the Line

Linen for Sale

England

We arrived in Hull on a typical English summer day, grey, drizzly and cool, but we were all so excited to have finally set foot in this legendary country, that it was of no consequence. There was a car (to make things even more exciting I think it was a Rolls Royce) which took us and our luggage to the train - for the final leg of our journey to London. It didn't occur to me then, but this was the same port that my father and his family had passed though from Poland en route to their new life in South Africa. I don't remember how long it took for us to reach London, but it was by far the shortest train journey I had ever made. Probably three or four hours. Going from Durban to Johannesburg took 13 hours and to Kimberley 23.

I stared out of the train window. I saw small green fields, cows and sheep grazing, towns whizzing past seemingly no distance apart. None of the vast open spaces I was accustomed to. The train slowed down as it chuffed through the outer suburbs of London, the back gardens of houses right up to the railway lines and some low buildings, probably factories. And then we were there.

In the taxi I asked, "Now where are we going?"

"Well, if you hadn't been so self absorbed you would have known."

"So, where?"

"We're going to stay at the Cumberland Hotel".

"Do you known where that is?"

"Not really, but we have been told that it is in the centre of London near Marble Arch and Oxford Street."

Well, I knew about Oxford Street from Monopoly. In fact all I really knew about London was from a few picture books and a lot of Monopoly. Oxford Street was red, and one of the better places to own and put up hotels, so that seemed a good place to be staying.

The Cumberland Hotel would become our base for the time my parents stayed in Europe, and mine until I found lodgings.

The first thing that struck me in the hotel, before even venturing out into Oxford Street or Park Lane, was the crowds milling around in the foyer. We had been on the ship for four weeks in a confined space with very few people, having left Durban, which after the end of the war and the repatriation of all the troops, had reverted to a small, quiet seaside town, so nothing had prepared me for these numbers. Being suddenly in a great crowded city was a shock.

The Cumberland Hotel itself was a luxurious palace. We were shown to our bedrooms, one for my parents and a double for Lorraine and me: hugely difference from sharing with four other women.

I asked my parents, "How is that we can suddenly afford this luxury?"

"Well, actually it's the only place we'd heard of."

When I think of it now, the whole trip must have taken an enormous amount of planning and preparation. Nowadays one just "logs on" and all the information is at hand but then there was almost nothing. I have no idea how they did it. In my usual way I had just left everything to them.

After unpacking and having a bath in fresh hot water with soap that lathered, (it doesn't in salt water) we hit the town.

"How do we get to Piccadilly Circus," we asked someone in the street.We wanted to see the lights, the multi-coloured flashing adverts.

"Oh, it's just around the corner, down Oxford Street, turn right into Regent Street and you're there."

We strolled along Oxford Street expecting all the time to see the right turn into Regent Street. It didn't seem to be there, but at length we reached it, turned right and continued walking.

"Something is wrong," my mother said, "That man said it was just around the corner."

So we stopped another passer-by.

"Yes, just down the road," was the answer.

It was a beautiful street but "Just around the corner? Just down the road?" How big was this city?

But it was worth it. Guinness, Bovril, Schweppes, Wrigleys and many more, all fought to be the brightest lights, the most dazzling, the most memorable. This is what we had come to see, but it was unexpectedly breathtaking. The fact that it was all just advertising was forgotten.

We weren't going to walk all that way back so we decided to do the iconic London thing: get a red bus.

We stood at the stop waiting for the bus to arrive. When it came, passengers got off, and then, just as we were stepping forward, before we could get on, the conductor shouted,

"Full up. Outside only."

We were already outside. What on earth did he mean? We didn't get on. Someone took pity on us.

"He means upstairs. The old buses didn't have a roof upstairs - so 'outside'. The expression has stuck."

We got on the next bus, and here was more unfathomable language. "How much is the fare?" my father asked

"Free ha'pence".

"Excuse me", from Issie

"Don't ya know? It's free harf pence, a penny hapenny. One an' a harf pennies."

We were going to have to learn a new language.

The plan was to see all the sights of London and then hire a car and travel the length and breadth of Britain before taking a coach trip to Europe. But first there was the important task, the main reason for us being in London - finding me a piano teacher. Gertie had written to two or three eminent pianists and teachers who had been recommended before we left Durban, and now appointments were made for my auditions.

"But I need somewhere to practise. I need to warm up." Suddenly I was very nervous. However, finding somewhere to practise proved quite easy because, "just around the corner" in Hanover Square, there were studios with pianos that could be rented by the hour.

I must admit that I don't remember the auditions. I have discovered that nerves, anxiety and stress play havoc with my memory. But I do remember playing to Illona Kabos, the person that Mr. and Mrs. Gerodi had suggested, and thinking that she would be just the teacher I needed. I was thrilled when she accepted me.

"She thinks you are really good," Gertie said. A bit of wishful thinking.

"I don't think so. All she said was that my pedaling was good. I suppose that is something,"

I wondered what that really meant. Anyway, I would be starting with her when we returned from the trip my father had organised, and when I had found somewhere to live. Actually everyone I played to was willing to teach me. My mother was convinced that they were all bowled over by my talent, but I now know, having myself taught in London for sixty years, that a talented person, willing to learn, and able to pay, is a prize most teachers are only too willing to accept.

Now that the dream of living in London without my family, on my own, was actually about to come true, I must have closed down all emotion, and my memory of the next few weeks is very sketchy, in fact, the European part of the trip is almost a complete blank. I was self-anaesthetised. However, I do remember seeing all the tourist spots in London, many of which I have never visited since. It was a grey, bleak and broken London. Bomb-sites were everywhere and there was no sign of restoration. Colour came only from the wild flowers which grew in abundance on the shattered ground. Nevertheless, there were huge crowds and long queues at every attraction. Life had returned to the people.

One of the reasons I have a rather worrying blank space where the Cooks Coach Tour of Europe should be, is that I really didn't want to go. I wanted to start my new life and I knew (or thought I knew) that I would be bored with the long coach journeys. Also, in retrospect, my memory loss is understandable. Underneath the very thin layer of sophisticated bravura behaviour, I must have been really fearful of the huge step I was taking.

The tour of Britain started as we set off in a rented car, my father driving, to visit as many towns and cities as time allowed. I remember visiting Stratford-on-Avon and seeing a Shakespeare play, and then I think we went straight on to Liverpool.

My mother's multitudinous family had been a joke amongst her friends. Someone once said that the first person to land on the moon (this was decades before anyone even contemplated such a thing) would be met by one of Gertie's relatives. But in England she only had one cousin - in Liverpool. Maurice Datnow. On our arrival there we found Maurice and his wife Elaine delightful and very welcoming. Later, their home would prove to be a haven for me. Maurice was a doctor, a gynaecologist obstetrician. Elaine's family owned furniture stores and they were willing to lend me a piano from one of the shops if I ever needed one. A god-send.

On the road once more, north to Scotland with a quick stop off at a very disappointing Gretna Green: a little hut on the border, not at all the romantic image for eloping couples I had conjured up.

Scotland was a culture shock. We couldn't understand a single word spoken to us. Cockney was bad enough but this was truly foreign. After freezing in Edinburgh, we made the return trip to the warmth and comfort of the Cumberland Hotel.

But not for long, it was time for the Cook's tour of Europe. I wasn't completely anaesthetised because I do remember being on the coach with a number of middle-aged people (I thought they were all ancient). I remember our first-ever sight of snow, on a mountain pass in Switzerland, and my father suddenly transforming into a ten year old boy, throwing snowballs at everyone.

I remember the outside of the cathedral in Milan and the religious souvenirs being sold on the streets, but that is all. Two weeks later we were back, and Issie and Lorraine were packing to return to Durban leaving Gertie and me to start our search for somewhere for me to live.

This was to prove much more difficult than we had anticipated. My mother wanted me to be with a nice Jewish family who would feed me and allow me to practise as much as necessary.

She suddenly remembered a couple who had come from Durban with their young daughter who was studying at the Royal Ballet School. So we went to their flat in Earls Court. I assumed it was for a visit, but Gertie was going to ask if I could stay with them. Well, that was out of the question. They had no spare room and no piano. We would have to continue hunting.

"Time is getting short," Gertie said. "You go and practise darling, (at the Hanover Studios) and I will find something."

All my life this had always been my get out. "You go and practise, darling, I'll do it". I had managed to avoid all sorts of unpleasant obligations so long as "I went and practised."

And so that is what I did, whilst she trudged the lonely streets of London. She came up with Queen Alexandra's House, which was student accommodation for the Royal College of Music. I think at the time it was only for girls and the whole atmosphere reminded me so much of school, that I felt I couldn't go there.

Back to the piano.

And then one day, in desperation, she walked into the WIZO (Women's International Zionist Organisation) building. She was a member of this movement back home. For her, being a Zionist meant raising money for the two-year-old State of Israel: somewhere for the displaced and dispossessed Jews, who had survived the Holocaust, to find peace. At the reception desk was a young woman who took a liking to Gertie and her plight.

"My mother has paying guests at our home in Muswell Hill," Enid said. "I'll speak to her. Normally she only has young men but I'll see what I can do."

St.Paul's Cathedral

Flowers in a bomb-site

Gretna Green

Issie and Lorraine with snowballs

Fourth Movement

Scherzo

Transformation

Piano Concerto - Lino-cut and mix media

Living In London

My mother and I were standing outside the front door of number 31 The Avenue, Muswell Hill - my heart thumping loudly.

The door opened, revealing a short round lady on high-heeled shoes, holding a shiny photograph in her hand.

"You must be Mrs. Israel and Anthya. I'm Dolly Lubel. Come in, come in," she said flapping the photo. Follow me."

Her shoes clanked across the tiled floor as she led us into her sitting room.

"Would you like a cup of tea?"

My mother would. I didn't drink tea.

"I'll leave you with this," she said handing over the shiny photo.

It wasn't a photo but a publicity leaflet for the young rising star in the musical firmament, Raymond Cohen, who had recently won the first International Carl Flesch Violin Competition.

Whilst Gertie studied the leaflet, I looked around the room. Nothing much to note really. A fireplace with a few pieces of coal, a rather shabby, worn sofa, and chairs and French windows to a somewhat unkempt garden. It would be OK.

Gertie had gone rather silent. Was that good or bad?

"Let me see it," I tried not to raise my voice. She handed over the brochure.

Mrs. Lubel's footsteps were clattering towards us so I took a quick glance.

Gorgeous, glamorous photo of a heartthrob young man with a violin. I could read my mother's mind: handsome; star; nice Jewish boy; hmmm. "I see you've looked at the picture," Mrs. Lubel said putting down the tea. Raymond has been here for the last two years. When I was working, it was useful, because he looked after the house."

"What? That gorgeous creature looking after the house?" I thought. "I don't believe her." Was she using him as a selling point? She didn't need to. I would probably be staying there, Raymond or not.

Whilst my mother sipped her tea, Mrs. Lubel told us what to expect from her boarding house.

She reiterated what Enid had told us, that I would be the first female lodger she had ever had and, with some prompting from Gertie, she listed what I could expect as a paying guest in her house.

I could have a piano in the front room.

I would have three kosher meals a day.

I would have to share a room with her younger daughter, Sylvia, but as soon as one of her regulars moved out, I would get a room of my own. Sylvia was at university, so not at home much.

I would give her my ration book.

I would pay her £4 weekly by cheque.

There was more, but I was having trouble taking it all in, and as it was in essence exactly what both of us had been looking for, and as no alternative had presented itself, we agreed to it all.

So now back to the Cumberland Hotel to organise everything.

The offer of a piano from the Datnows in Liverpool was gratefully accepted and arrangements made for its delivery to no.31.

Two things I had never needed before were a bank account and a coat.

I had never owned or worn a coat so this was exciting. In England rationing of clothes had just come to an end and what was now available was called "Utility". I think there were top fashion-house clothes available but only for the very rich. However, I managed to find a Utility winter coat in cobalt blue, which I loved. It looked great, until the first time it came into contact with rain, when it stretched downwards, and the hem had a mind of its own from then on.

I had never had a bank account or written a cheque. It hadn't been necessary. I had been given money for bus fares or small treats when I needed it. Now my difficulty with numbers (no maths ability and at that time no calculators) would have to be remedied.

My weekly allowance was £10. £4 for Mrs. Lubel, £4 for

Illona Kabos and £2 for me.

Time slipped by and I found myself back at no.31 saying goodbye to my mother who was flying home to South Africa, an adventure for her, which would involve stopping overnight at various African towns on the way, for refuelling, and some sleep for the crew.

Perhaps I should have been fearful of what awaited me in this strange house filled with unknown people, and even more fearful of the gigantic, completely unknown city, but I had psychologically prepared myself for this adventure and was determined to enjoy it.

There was a lot to explore.

No. 31 was a terraced house; something I had never seen before, joined on both sides to the next-door houses. From the outside it was really hard to tell which was which, but number 31 had a blue front door, so that was its distinguishing feature.

It was almost at the top of The Avenue and the terraced houses continued down Duke's Avenue at right angles to The Avenue. I loved the way they appeared to skip hand-in hand up and down the hilly road. Later that year, when it snowed, I thought it was truly beautiful, although other members of the household were not nearly so impressed.

From The Avenue, one could see the back of Alexandra Palace, a huge, grey, lumbering edifice, not a beautiful fairytale palace, but it was surrounded by an enormous leafy park, and no. 31 faced the park on the opposite side of the road.

This was a joy because, over the year, I could watch the four changing seasons. I had only known summer and winter: spring and autumn were a revelation. In autumn the leaves changing from green to yellow and red and falling to cover the pavements, enabled me to swish through their crackling brown remains, like paddling on the beach. Spring was not just buds and fresh yellow-green foliage appearing, but there was a change in the light and a lengthening of the days. I could have lived without the cold, short, dark winter days - it's the light I missed (I still do), but the long, long summer evenings were completely unexpected and wonderful. Twilight and dusk were poetical words I had read and never understood. In Durban there was no such thing as lingering light after the sun had set. When the sun went down over the horizon, it was quite suddenly dark.

Walking along hilly Dukes Avenue brought me to the centre of Muswell Hill. The Odeon Cinema was here, and this is where I could get a bus into the city. But apart from a little shop which sold newspapers and confectionary, where once a month I would exchange my sweet coupons for two small paper bags of tempting treats, the area was shabby and run-down, and there was nothing to buy.

Except for my first brief visit to no.31, I had never been inside a house like it before. It looked so small from the outside but, as if in an Alice in Wonderland world, it grew, spreading back - on and on.

Opening the front door you enter a dark, long, rather narrow corridor with a staircase directly ahead. On the left at the bottom of the stairs, is a small table with a phone. On the table is a notebook with a pencil attached to it by a length of string. I guess I will have to make a note of any phone calls I make.

On the right is the dining room. A large, high-ceilinged room, fully equipped for formal meals. This is where my piano is, so I will be spending a lot of time there. Further along the corridor, on the right is the sitting room that I knew from my first visit. Onwards and down a few steps is the morning room. Here there is a table big enough to seat eight to ten people, wooden chairs and a sideboard filled with cutlery and crockery. This is where all the meals will be eaten.

Through the door at the back of the room is the kitchen: a small room with a window and a door to the garden, and something else new to me - a gas cooker. I had never seen or used gas before, everything in South Africa was electric. Thank goodness I won't have to do any cooking.

Back out of the morning room, down the passage, and up the stairs. This house grows upwards as well. My room is up yet another set of stairs: right at the top, the attic. I will be sharing this bedroom with Sylvia Lubel. I hope I like her.

It's a large room, the ceiling quite low, two windows with no curtains, two single beds covered with red and blue eiderdowns, two wardrobes, two chests of drawers, and beside my bed (the one on the left), a small rug on the lino covered floor, and a bedside table. There isn't a lamp on this table, only a light hanging from the ceiling in the middle of the room.

Back down the stairs to the first floor: the front room is Mrs Lubel's bedroom and the far back room is Raymond's. Next to it is the bathroom with a basin, a bath and another new thing, a geyser on the wall to provide hot water. There is a separate WC with the lavatory pan at one end of a long, narrow room. There are more bedrooms, but I never get to see any of them.

So what about the people who live in this house? There is, of course, Mrs Lubel herself, the mother of three grown-up children who are all still living at home. Enid is the oldest, in her late twenties, plump and short like her mother but, unlike her, she is blond and pretty. Enid is the reason I am here in this house. It was she who persuaded her mother, after meeting Gertie at the Women's International Zionist Organisation, to have me as her first female paying guest. Sylvia is the youngest sibling. She too is short but very slim and very highly-strung. She is reading history at Bristol University and has a boyfriend who plays all the popular songs by ear in the key of B flat! He doesn't live at no.31 but is a constant visitor. Monte is the spoiled boy of the family, his mother's pride and joy, especially as he is studying to be a doctor. Later, when Enid meets and marries a doctor, a major in uniform, very smart and elegant, Mrs Lubel's Jewish ambitions are fulfilled. Three doctors in the family. Who could ask for more?

And then there are a changing number of young men, all Jewish, all students and all destined to become successful professors, lawyers, architects, and in one case a musician.

(Not Raymond, who is already a successful musician. A lot more of him later.)

Now I had to settle down to living and working here. Although every thing was different, I still had to get up every morning, have breakfast and start practising. There were rules about how much and how long I could use the piano. I had to stop every evening by six o'clock and there was no music on Saturdays or on Jewish Holidays. Not only did Mrs.Lubel forbid this, but she was also very concerned not to upset her very orthodox neighbours. Lunch was at one o'clock, in the morning room, quite often with Raymond, who would have been playing his violin in his room. This was wonderful because it gave me the chance to get to know him and learn more about his life than I had read in his brochure. I already knew that he was thirty-one years old, had spent six years in the Royal Corp of Signals Band during the war and then, whilst still in uniform, had won the first Carl Flesch International Violin Competition. The result of this was that he was becoming one of the most well-known and admired violinists in Europe. So I was quite shy and somewhat in awe of him. But that soon vanished. He had no airs and graces and loved to make me laugh. When he wasn't doing solo concerts, he led various orchestras including the BBC Television Orchestra.

At that time the BBC television studios were in Alexandra Palace, just up the road. It was built in 1879 as "a centre for recreation and entertainment," and was known (as it still is) to all Londoners as Ally Pally. Although very few people owned television sets in 1950/51, television was beamed from its 215ft transmission tower and once a week there were live variety shows with all sorts of acts and some musical items conducted by Eric Robinson.

At that time there wasn't a TV set at the Lubels, but I became very intrigued by the stories Raymond told of the goings on at Ally Pally. So I plucked up courage and persuaded him to invite me to a rehearsal and a show. I was expecting a slick professional performance but was amazed to discover how make-shift everything was. The disorder at the rehearsal made me think of a primary school concert. Artists tripped over the cables streaming across the floor as they looked for the chalk marks indicating where they were to stand. Electricians clambered in and out of the lights on the ceiling, moving them around and calling down for approval from the producers. Two large cameras, manned by two or three men rolled backwards and forwards and it all looked chaotic. As this was to be a live performance I was sure it would be a disaster.

The show started almost immediately after the rehearsal ended. Large placards with the names of the next item on the programme were held up in front of the small audience, as were the signs for laughter and applause. A charming, very lady-like announcer, in a beautiful dress, sat at a table on one side, and in a cut-glass accent announced the next item.

After each item Eric Robinson turned from the orchestra, beamed at the cameras and said a few rather incoherent words, whilst behind him scurrying men changed the background for the next performer. And then it was over, and everyone disappeared until the following week when the whole disarray would be repeated.

Back to my everyday life: after lunch I would go back to the piano, spending the next three or four hours trying to achieve a standard that would satisfy Miss Kabos.

During my first few days, Mrs. Lubel gave me a few more rules to follow. My guess about the book on the telephone table was correct: any call I made had to be timed, noted and paid for.

A certain amount of maths ability was required for this task as the price of phone-calls varied depending on the time of day, or the day of the week, or the length of the call. Phoning after six pm and on Sundays was the cheapest. As I hardly knew anyone, this was not going to cost me much. As we were not allowed to make trunk calls (those made to places out of London), the red phone-box just across the road was used for those. International calls were hugely expensive and difficult to make: a time for them had to be booked via an operator, and in the two years I lived there whilst my parents were in Durban, they never once phoned. A three minute call would have cost as much as two weeks rent.

Raymond was a frequent occupant of the red phone-box. He was very fond of his mother, and after his father died, felt very sorry for her, so once a week or so her would phone home to Manchester. He had developed a method of making the phone call last as long as possible without having to pay over the odds, and was very pleased with himself for stumbling upon this ruse.

He would dial 0, tell the operator what number he wanted and she would tell him how much money he needed to insert in coins. Having put in the coins, he would press button A, and be put through. After talking for the allotted time (usually 3 minutes) the operator would interrupt the conversation.

"Your time is up, caller."

"Just finishing up operator," he would say and go on talking.

This could happen a number of times during the call, so his three minutes could sometimes stretch into nine or ten.

Another rule in the house was the bathing regulations. There was a written rota for when and how you could have a bath. I was allocated a bath once a week in 5 inches of water. During the war, this was a government restriction, but whether it still was, or just Mrs. L saving money on heating the water, I don't know. In any case I was pleased that I didn't have to face the fearsome water heater more than once a week. In order to get hot water, the very large geyser on the wall had to be lit with a match. I was terrified of it, so I held the match at its very end and then jumped back as fast as I could. If I was lucky and it took, it would roar and explode into action. The hot water would then dribble into the bath and I was glad of only five inches. More would have taken all day.

The lavatory was in a separate room next door, and here there was rationing of paper. I think toilet-paper was still officially rationed. Occasionally there was that hard stuff that came in a box and at number 31 it was augmented with torn up pages of the Radio Times. One of the boarders joked that he only used pages from Radio 3 - the classical music programme. I begged my parents to send me rolls of the best toilet paper available in South Africa. Its arrival was even more welcome that the regular large, round tins of Quality Street sweets, sent by my Aunt Frieda. Although I shared the sweets with everyone in the house, nobody got my toilet paper.

In retrospect, it is difficult for me to imagine how my parents brought themselves to leave me in London, this unknown, enormous city. In her numerous letters to me, my mother expressed much concern about my health (was I wearing a warm vest etc.) but my safety was never questioned. They knew no more than a couple of people in London, but having found me a safe haven in Muswell Hill, they didn't give me one word of warning. It is hard to understand how or why this was, except perhaps that they were too embarrassed, or really too ignorant of life in a swarming city 6000 miles away. Durban was a tiny village in comparison. I, of course, loved the freedom and probably, because of my own innocence, was completely unafraid. Except for the occasion when I was stopped one day at a tube station, by a tall imposing black man who asked me for directions. This was the first time a black man who was a stranger (not someone's servant) had ever spoken to me. I was startled and a little frightened. I did manage to tell him how to get to Bond Street Station but, on reflection, my initial reaction of alarm appalled me. I hadn't realised how deep the instilled fear had penetrated my mind.

Publicity photo of Raymond

174

Alexandra Palace from the top of The Avenue

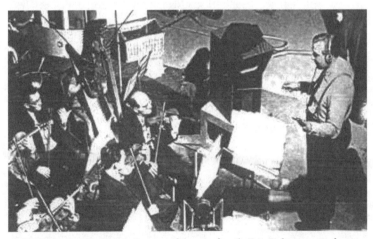

BBC Television Orchestra. Raymond (centre front), Eric Robinson conducting

Life At Number 31

My piano practice would stop at about six pm. Then at seven, all the residents of the Lubel house would meet around the dinner table in the morning room. I thought that Mrs. Lubel was a really good cook, managing to conjure up very tasty meals for her family and paying guests, in spite of the severe rationing.(Food rationing did not end until 1953). She did, of course, have a lot of ration books from all of us residents, and that must have helped.

As everything in my life now was unfamiliar, living with people who were all much older than me was, at first, difficult. I was shy and unsure of myself. The fact that so many of them were young men made it harder and I found myself chattering inanely as a cover-up. After dinner, those of us who had no other commitments would gather in the sitting room. In the winter everyone huddled as near as possible to the small flicker of flames from the rather miserable coal fire which was meant to warm the room. (Coal was still severely rationed.)

I soon learned that sitting close burned the front of my legs but left the rest of me freezing.

Some of the conversation which was generated at the dining table, now continued on more comfortable chairs and sofas. War was present in everyone's mind, especially as the Korean War had started in October 1950 and those students, who would have to do two years of National Service in the forces when they graduated from university, were very worried that they would be called up to serve. And so, politics was a common theme of the evening discussions.

Despite my shyness, I loved being part of what I considered to be intellectual debate. My strong point was knowledge of South Africa, especially the emerging horrors of Apartheid. Most of this was unknown to the others: South African politics only hit the headlines some years later. Most of the residents were strongly left wing and one man, Sid, was an ardent member of the Communist Party. He had a habit of standing, legs akimbo, in front of the fire, blocking out the little heat, whilst spouting his theories. I couldn't put Communism and Sid together.

Another frequently recurring topic of discussion was religion. We were all Jewish, but of radically different levels of belief and practice. During one of these discussions, Monte Lubel let slip that he was seeing Mary, who was a fellow student at the hospital where he was studying. Everyone was very pleased for him until he said,

"She's not Jewish."

"Gosh! Your mother isn't going to like that," someone said.

"Of course, that's my predicament. I don't know what to do."

This problem became one of the main topic of argument and deliberation for months to come as Monte fell more and more deeply in love with Mary. Their relationship took some years to resolve, but the story has a happy ending: they finally married and "lived happily ever after" in Southend-on-Sea where Monte had a GP practice.

I began to realise how completely spoiled, pampered and protected I had been at home. Because it was a "nice" Jewish middle class home, I had never heard a swear word, never discussed sex, and the few friends I had wouldn't have dreamed of doing that. But I had read a lot of books, and what I considered "dirty" words did occur there, so I knew their meaning. Now in Muswell Hill, in the real world, I think that the young men respected my naivety and youth and behaved impeccably, until one evening we decided to play the old fashioned game of Consequences. It goes something like this:

Write a story. On a sheet of paper write one section of the story. Then fold the paper and pass it on. Here are the sections 1) A description beginning with the word 'the', e.g. 'The beautiful', 'The very talkative', 2) A man's name, 3) A second description, as above, 4) A woman's name, 5) Where they met, 6) What he gave her, 7) What she said, 8) What he said, 9) What the consequence was, Read it all aloud.

Our version was all perfectly innocent until "the consequence was" was read out, Gonorrhoea, Raymond had written. Every one laughed, except me. (Nowadays every schoolboy would write that.) I was horrified. How could he? What sort of man was this? That was not a word to be spoken out loud. Now, remembering my reaction, I am flabbergasted at how I felt, but I am still conscious of the almost electric shock I felt then. It took me some time to accept what I supposed could be called "adult" language. Later I discovered that Raymond too had been shocked when he first went into the army, at the language he heard there. He never learned to smoke or to drink in the six years he spent there, but he did learn all the four-letter words and did not hesitate to use them.

For the first few months of my stay everyone treated me as a little mascot from darkest Africa.

I certainly got teased about my accent. No one around had ever heard it before and they were all determined to tone it down. I would regularly announce that I was going bed to write the obligatory letter home and it was always met with,

"Oh! So you are going to write leeters in beed".

It became a catch phrase in the house.

A blue airmail letter from my mother would arrive for me at least twice a week, and I was supposed to answer all the questions put to me. Was I wearing a warm vest? Had I been to see "so-and-so," one of the handful of friends she had made during her stay in London. When was Miss Kabos going to arrange concerts for me? Later there were a lot of questions about Raymond and what sort of relationship I was making with him. She also filled me in on all the musical activities of the young people I had known back home: who had won which prize and who had played at which event or concert. I had lost all interest in them. It all seemed like another world. However at least once a week I had to write home to fill her in with some news and a few white lies, and the only warm place to do so, was in bed.

My bedroom was not in any other way inviting. There were two temperatures in the room: either swelteringly hot (there were no curtains at the windows) or freezing cold, so cold, that the water in the glass at my bedside froze solid over-night. There was a free-standing one-bar gas fire which could be lit when I came upstairs and extinguished on getting into bed, but, like the electric fire in the room with the piano, it was little better than useless. However, under the bedclothes it was warm, and in winter I would dress and undress cowering under the blankets and eiderdown.

In the summer of 1951 I was incarcerated for two weeks in my bedroom. I had caught chicken pox. It was the hottest two weeks of the year and I was covered from head to foot in excruciatingly itchy spots. They were everywhere: in my hair, in my mouth and down my throat. Agony. Monte, the son of the house, was taking his final medical exams, and the fear that he would catch my deadly disease permeated the house. Three times a day the door would open a crack and my food would be left on the floor. It really was imprisonment. Raymond who was away most of that time, had phoned his mother to ask if he had ever had chickenpox. She couldn't remember, so occasionally he would put his head round the door, come in, stand as close to the door as possible, and have a little chat, better than nothing, but finally I decided that enough was enough, hid the remaining spots under make up and clothes, and ventured downstairs to my neglected piano.

Life in the Lubel house was never boring. There was a lot of tension in the family. A lot of shouting and loud quarrelling, which created a febrile atmosphere. There was also a secret, a skeleton in the cupboard, which could have been the underlying cause of the friction.

Mr. Lubel, the father of the three children and, no doubt, at one time Mrs.L's husband, was never mentioned. Where was he? What had happened to him? Mrs. L talked proudly and often of her brother, who was of course a doctor, the local Muswell Hill doctor, but not a word was spoken of a husband or father. The children never let a word slip and there were no photos of them together in happier days. So when none of the family was around, there was a lot of lurid speculation amongst the lodgers as to where and when and how he had disappeared. How bad could the reason be? Had he run off with a young shiksa? (A rude word for a non-Jewish girl). Had he developed a dreadful sexually transmitted disease and been isolated? I liked my theory best - Mrs. Lubel had murdered him. That would cover all the possibilities. During the time I lived there, I realised how angry, bad-tempered and out of control she could get, and began to believe she really was capable of murder when, one day I became the butt of her fury.

I had been practising for seven or eight months on the upright piano that the Datnow family had lent me. I was very lucky to have had it, but it was becoming more and more apparent to me that I needed something better, something that would help me to create all the different qualities and quantities of sound that the works I was now learning required.

One day when a friend, Benjamin Kaplan, a fellow music student, who lived near by, told me that he had bought a new piano and asked me if I would like to buy his small grand, I was very excited. But I couldn't just agree. There were many questions to be asked and many arrangements to be made. First I had to get permission from Mrs. L.

"How would you feel about me getting rid of my piano and getting a small grand piano instead? I'm afraid it would take up more space in your room."

"I'll think about it," she said. To my surprise and delight she was quite pleased.

"I think it would look nice in there. Go ahead."

I was expecting it to be more difficult.

Would my parents buy it for me? Letters went to and fro.

"Yes, do," was the answer, "We could use it if we decide to come to London."

This was all going well.

The next stage was logistics. Neither Ben nor I could possibly be without a piano for more than a few hours, so we made a plan. His old piano would be moved out of his house, and his new piano moved in. My upright would be sent back to Liverpool, and his grand would take its place. All on the same morning. One Thursday morning, all this would come about.

We were very pleased with ourselves.

But: I had left Mrs. Lubel out of the loop. I had forgotten to tell her that this was going to happen on Thursday morning. She went ballistic. Thursday was her market day and she wasn't going to let anyone move anything into or out of her house if she wasn't present to oversee it. She was incandescent with rage, purple in the face, and screaming, and I, who had never ever lost my temper before, felt the blood boiling in my veins.

" I'm really sorry, but it's absolutely impossible to change all these arrangements," I tried to tell her. "I promise to make sure that no damage is done to any of the walls."

Nothing calmed her down.

"They will be in and out of here in half an hour. Could you go to the market later?"

More yelling.

I was by now crying.

And then Raymond (a knight in shining armour) arrived on the scene. Somehow he managed to quieten her enough to tell her that he would supervise the move. And suddenly she was silent. She grabbed her bag and clattered out of the house. I, on the other hand, took days to get over it.

The room in which all this drama took place was officially the dining room of the house. It was a large room with high ceilings, and during winter it never warmed up. I doubt if it had been warm for fifty years. I was given a small electric radiator that I could switch on when I entered the room and had to switch off immediately on leaving. I put it as close to me as possible, but it had little or no effect, particularly on the ivory piano keys, which are notoriously impossible to heat. Nothing does it, not even a hot water bottle placed on them. It is almost impossible to play with cold hands, so I practised in fingerless gloves, but that didn't stop me getting terrible chilblains on my fingers. They were red, cracked and painful and when they got so bad that I could no longer play, I used to invite myself to the cousins in Liverpool, Maurice and Elaine Datnow. They had a beautiful big, blissfully centrally heated house, surrounded by a large garden, and they took great care of me. The piano they had lent me from one of their shops had been returned, but I was full of guilt because I had singed the wood on the treble side by having the fire too close. They were completely unconcerned.

Maurice was a gynaecologist and obstetrician and a very keen gardener. He had been brought up on a farm in South Africa (the farm we used to visit when we were in Kimberley). Elaine was English (from Newcastle I think) and was a passionate bridge player. She shocked my seventeen-year-old self by asking me if I played bridge.

"No".

"Well, you must," she said. "You will never get into society if you don't".

I still don't play bridge. I do not want to "get into" that society, whatever it may be.

Both Maurice and Elaine were Jewish, but they led, what I thought of, as a very upper-class English life. Their three boys all went to boarding school from a very early age, and seemed to me, to be completely detached from their mother and father. When they were home on holiday they treated them with extreme politeness, almost as though they were strangers. Very alien to me. That was another thing I was not going to "get into."

Maurice was giving me a lift to the station in his car one day, when he started to complain about the National Health Service. Fortunately, until then, I had not needed any medical attention in London and so hadn't given the NHS a second thought, simply taken it for granted. I assumed that everyone was really happy that they were getting free medical treatment and I believed that doctors would be equally delighted to give it. Surely, the NHS was an integral part of life in England. Listening to Maurice grumbling about it was a surprise. He wasn't criticising the way it was run, but about the formation of it. It had been launched in July 1948 so it was only two years old, and Maurice, (along with many other doctors), was doubtful whether he would be able to retain his private patients and his good income. His fears were groundless. He did work for the NHS in a hospital in Liverpool, but continued to have a flourishing private practice.

It took four hours by train to Liverpool from London in those days. A very short journey to me. One day, returning to London, I sat opposite a miserably distressed woman.

"What's the matter?" I asked her

"I haven't been to London before," she sobbed.

That was a shock to me. How was that possible when London was so near?

"I'm going to see my daughter who lives there, it's such a long way away," she told me, twisting her handkerchief into knots and wiping her eyes.

Years later, I learned that there were people living in the far-flung suburbs of London who never ventured into the city.

Back in Muswell Hill, it was not only the Lubel family who made life interesting, but some of the lodgers had their own odd quirks. There was Daniel, who was wont to inform us all that he was going to post a letter. This was of no interest until we would notice, after some days, that he was not around. A week or so later he would return, sit down to dinner and later relax in the sitting room, with not a word spoken of his disappearance. Once he was gone for two weeks, but still no one had any idea what he was up to.

As I have already mentioned, there was Sid, the Communist, spouting his deeply held theories of sharing and equality, and behaving in exactly the opposite manner, hogging all the heat of the fire. We were all so ridiculously polite that no one stopped him causing the rest of us to freeze. It was a hard-won way of learning about politics.

Julius was a serious Social Science student. He was small, dark, and wore thick horn-rimmed spectacles and smoked a pipe. He looked and behaved, aged twenty-one, as if he was already the professor he was later to become. All his opinions were carefully thought through and perfectly enunciated.

Malcolm, a student viola player, was in many ways the exact opposite. Although he too was dark haired, his was almost black, shiny with Brylcreem, and swept back over his ears and touching his collar. He would not have been seen dead in the tweed jacket Julius sported, but somehow managed to look "artistic" wearing a collection of colourful clothes. He was ahead of his time in many ways. He was from Manchester (as was Raymond), and, having completed his Army National Service, had realised that, as he was never going to be more than a second rate violinist, he would become a viola player. (A second rate viola player?) So now he was studying in London and was staying at the Lubels to be near to his idol, Raymond, and pick up as many musical and technical tips as he could. Over the next few months, he somehow assumed the role of resident critic. He would go to, or listen to, every performance Raymond gave, and having become very cocky and self assured, take it on himself to inform Raymond of what he, Malcolm, thought would improve his performance.

I was shocked. "What does he say", I asked, "He would like everything exaggerated. Louder, faster, me moving around more. He's an idiot".

Raymond hated it, and was very relieved when Mrs. L asked Malcolm to leave. He had been criticising her as well. A big mistake.

However, Malcolm's self-belief stood him in good stead. He somehow managed to persuade Sir John Barbirolli to give him a position as one of the violas of the Halle Orchestra, where he stayed for some years.

And Raymond? He will get a chapter to himself.

I have forgotten exactly when technology entered no.31, but one day a television set arrived. It was a large piece of dark wood furniture with a small square glass window. There was only one programme to watch, beamed from Ally Pally; just up the road. Whilst the rest of England suffered from very intermittent pictures and much moving of aerials, here it came over clear and strong. I don't remember watching it much, it was not until 1953 with the coronation of Queen Elizabeth, that millions of people became hooked on television.

And then Raymond added to the technology boom. He became the proud possessor of a very large, very heavy,

Ferrograph reel-to-reel tape recorder. These were not generally available, but one of his friends in the TV world had pulled a few strings. With a lot of heaving and shoving it was installed in his bedroom. It was there mainly to record from the radio the broadcasts he was doing, but it was a great toy, and we were all enjoying recording our voices and listening to them in disbelief.

"That's not how I sound," everyone said. One day he recorded Mrs. Lubel ranting about something in the hall below and played it back at its highest volume. She recognised the words but not the voice, and came rampaging up the stairs, heels stamping loudly.

"How dare you. I will not be treated like this," she yelled.

We were all doubled up with suppressed laughter, and it took a long time to convince her that it was her own voice.

Then one day Raymond turned on the machine and, without any apparent reason, out came a conversation between two people. This was truly eerie. Where was it coming from? He tried pressing all sorts of buttons but still the voices were there. Then an idea dawned,

"Let's go and see what's on the television at this moment," he said.

And there on the set were two people having the same conversion we could hear on the tape recorder. The signal from Ally Pally was so strong that it was coming directly from the socket in the wall.

Illona Kabos

I took two buses to get to Illona Kabos for my piano lessons in Park Road near to Bakers Street. One bus to Golders Green (the 102), and then a choice of number 2 or 13. It took about an hour, even in those days when there was very little traffic. The second bus took me past Finchley Road Station and past a little shop which sold coffee beans. They roasted the beans there and the air was filled with the most delicious aroma. I didn't even drink coffee in those days but to this day (I do drink it now), I still think the smell is even better than the taste. Finchley Road led to Swiss Cottage where both sides of the road were littered by remains of bombed out houses, some still had one wall standing, showing the wallpaper and decorations of the ghost rooms.

Illona's flat, which was on the ground floor of a mansion block, was still in perfect condition. My lessons took place in a very large room occupying a corner of the building, me at the grand piano and Miss Kabos ensconced on a sofa within easy reach of her telephone, on which she would quite often have long conversations in Hungarian. The only word I picked up was "Igen" which I believe is "yes". She used it a lot.

She was a very beautiful, petite woman, with delicate features, upswept blond hair and huge eyes. I thought she was very old, but actually she was in her fifties. She had small but very strong hands, strong enough to be able to perform all the main repertoire. At that time she was renowned for her performances of the Liszt and Bartok concertos which she had played to Bartok himself in her native Hungary. She studied and taught at the Franz Liszt Academy of Music before coming to London with her then husband, the pianist Louis Kentner. They were divorced before I knew her.

Miss Kabos was the perfect teacher for me, taking me from student to a performing artist.

My first lesson was a wake up call.

"Play me some Scarlatti, please." I had never played Scarlatti.

"Well, which Chopin Etude can you play?" I didn't know any.

I had virtually no repertoire. I had spent eight years taking one exam a year, playing one concerto and learning show-off pieces. I had learned one Beethoven sonata and one Bach Prelude and Fugue but that was the limit of my classical repertoire.

It was disastrous and very embarrassing.

"Well, darlink," Miss Kabos said. "We have a lot of work to do."

To begin with I had to alter my finger technique which I had thought was quite good.

"Darlink. Relax your hands. They look like claws," she proclaimed. She was never polite for the sake of it.

"Practise all these scales, some Hanon finger exercises and a Czerny study."

These were not the scales that I could rattle off whilst reading a book. These were much more complex.

"And learn this Schubert Impromptu, I will hear it next week."

That was my first lesson.

A week later, I played the Schubert to her.

"No, no, no, darlink. I want performance not hesitant unlearned rubbish. Go home, learn it properly and play it from memory. Also get the music for Bach's Italian Concerto, learn the first movement and I will hear both of them next week."

Wow! This was new. It had taken weeks for me to learn anything before. I was forced to find out how to practise properly. It was a great gift. There wasn't time for futile repetitions, going over and over a difficult passage hoping that somehow it would eventually come right. Now I had to concentrate on getting every section understood and perfected. After a while, scales and exercises slipped out of the scene, but the things that were to remain vital in my life as a musician followed. She taught me how to produce variations in sound quality giving me the technical means, not only for dynamics, but how to make the beautiful or hard or delicate qualities that I had always wanted to do. She also brought me out of my shell.

"Darlink! More! More!"

She scrawled with huge gestures across my music, sometimes in red pencil.

Every now and again she would invite all her pupils, about eight of us, to perform to each other and we would have to give our opinion on each person before she gave her verdict. This was the scariest and sometimes the most embarrassing thing. At that stage of my development they all sounded wonderful and I could never think of anything to criticise, but it did teach me how to listen critically and not just be amazed at technical proficiency.

Sometimes she invited a guest to come to these "master classes", and I think that it was through one of these people that I was invited to give a recital in aid of a charity at a private home. It went well, and two or three other events followed. It was a good beginning to what I hoped would be my career in England.

As I was not allowed to practise on Saturdays or after about six in the evenings, I was able to take full advantage of musical life in London. A small booklet, which was the 1950's version of "Time Out", listed all the concerts, opera, and theatres that interested me. What I saw amazed me. Every day there were at least seven concerts that I could choose between. Seven! In Durban there was one a week. Where to start?

Somehow I found myself at an evening for young musicians at the Commonwealth Club. Here, to my dismay, I found myself listening to people who were discussing the merits and faults of various operas they had seen. I had never been to an opera, so I felt that, in order to be an educated musician, I had to get there as soon as possible. The brilliant thing about the Commonwealth Club was that they always had free tickets for events and I grabbed a ticket to see Wagner's "Lohengrin" and sat through five hours in the gods. I did see some other operas, but the standard in those days was not great and I found myself too often getting the giggles at the silly stories and the terrible acting.

There were also tickets to concerts and I went to as many as I could. The Queen's Hall, which had been the favourite London concert venue, had been bombed and so concerts took place at the Royal Albert Hall with its renowned echo acoustic, or in various theatres and in many churches, as well as the Wigmore Hall, Conway Hall and Westminster Hall.

And then in May 1951 the Royal Festival Hall was opened on the South Bank of the Thames. It was the focal point of the "Festival of Britain" which had been conceived as an attempt to give the people of Britain a feeling of recovery, although much of London was still in ruins: redevelopment had not even started. It was planned to display the arts, architecture, science, technology and industrial design and was full of colour and strange edifices such as the Skylon, a huge rocket shaped object which appeared to hang in space.

I managed to get a ticket to the Festival Hall quite soon after it opened to hear the violinist Yehudi Menuhin and his pianist sister Hephzibah give a recital. I sat in the twelfth row and was bowled over by how close to the stage it seemed, the racked seats giving a clear view and seeming to bring the stage nearer to the audience. The hall itself was in every way astonishing. The first "modern" building I had ever been in and, I think, one of the first new buildings in London. I quite agreed with the journalist Bernard Levin who wrote:

"I was overwhelmed by a shock of breathless delight at the originality and beauty of the interior. It felt as if I had been instantly transported far into the future and that I was on another planet,"

It has ever since been the main London concert hall and, although the acoustics have always been problematic, it is still a wonderful venue.

I went to the RFH whenever I could afford to. I had been to many concerts in Durban, but somehow, either because the orchestra didn't play many complete symphonies, or because I hadn't been to the right concerts, I had hardly any knowledge of orchestral music. This struck me forcibly at a London concert when a Brahms symphony was being played. I knew that it wasn't modern or discordant, in fact it was a beautiful sound, but it made no sense to me, just a jumble of notes. I was quite ashamed of this and decided to listen to Brahms on the radio as much as possible. I didn't listen very closely, just let the music seep into me. And then, listening more intently one day, an epiphany occurred! A light switched on. Exactly like that. Seeing (or hearing) the light, suddenly it all made sense. The phrases and harmonies fell into place like pieces of a jigsaw coming together. It was a weird and exciting experience.

Raymond And Me

After I had been in Muswell Hill for a few months, things stopped being strange and unfamiliar and I became aware that my attention was becoming more and more focused on Raymond. It was difficult to avoid this because he was around a lot. We had lunch together when he was at home whilst everyone else was out, and enjoyed talking "music" together. Although our backgrounds seemed to be so different, our religious and political feelings were very much in tune, as our musical ones would become in time. He had been quite sceptical about my pianistic abilities when I first arrived and he heard me practising scales and studies and having difficulties with the different technique which my new teacher demanded. He told one or two people, that surely I should have been more advanced before making the perilous six thousand mile journey. He himself was virtually born playing the violin and didn't remember having to go through that stage, but, as my playing quickly improved, he saw the talent beneath the struggle, and began to ask me to play with him, especially music which was new to him.

So we had become friends and I found him very attractive and realised that I was falling in love with him. I don't know at which point he recognised that I was no longer a plump little girl and had become a slim and sexually mature young woman, but it took time for him to overcome his anxiety over the fourteen-year age difference between us. In any case, he was being pursued, as a very eligible bachelor, by older and more sophisticated women.

In the meantime I was learning a great deal about the violin and violin playing. Quite soon after my arrival at no.31 he asked whether I could do him a favour: stand outside his closed bedroom door whilst he played three different violins, one after the other, and tell him which one sounded best. I didn't understand what all this was about, but it turned out that he needed a better violin than the one he was at present playing.

"My fiddle is really not good enough and I'm having to borrow one whenever I do important concerts. Let's hope one of these will fit the bill".

"Why am I standing outside the door?" I asked.

"Well, you won't be able to see which violin is which and perhaps will get a completely unbiased opinion."

He obviously didn't realise that it would be a completely uninformed opinion.

I was very embarrassed. They all sounded beautiful, after all, he was playing them, and to my untrained ears they all sounded exactly the same.

It took time and experience, but I eventually become expert at differentiating. I was to hear countless numbers over the years.

Raymond was obsessed with the violin and violin playing. Not only his own, but the playing of all other violinists, particularly those for whom he had great admiration. He would twiddle about on the radio in his room until he could hear the sounds he was listening for, and then get very excited if it was one of his favourites. Now he wanted to share this enthusiasm and would shout from his room,

"Come and listen to this, its Heifetz," (Jasha Heifetz was his god) or sometimes David Oistrach from Russia, or any number of other names from obscure radio stations. Of course I went, but I could hear nothing except a thick fog of static. He had developed selective hearing. He thought that the radio he now had was wonderful, such a vast improvement over the Crystal set he had as a child.

I sometimes asked him to tell me things about his childhood. He always said he couldn't remember anything. I, who had just left my childhood, found that strange. He was happy to tell me odd things about the six years he had spent in the army.

"I hated every moment," he said. "What I hated most was never being in control, always being told what to do."

He was 19 years old when he was called up, and spent the first few months in the Royal Corps of Signals, square bashing, and being trained as a wireless operator. After some months he was sent home on embarkation leave, expecting that when he returned to camp, he would be sent to the Far East. Instead, to his amazement and relief, he read on a notice board that he had been transferred to the Royal Corp of Signals Band. There he was given a clarinet to play. He had never played a clarinet before, but after a lesson or two was considered proficient enough to join the military band on parade and in bandstands. But there was also an orchestra that needed string players to play for the entertainment of the officers and for dances and even public concerts. Raymond was pleased to discover other former students of the Northern College of Music in the band. He was almost immediately appointed the leader of the orchestra and was often called upon for solo items. The war was not yet over when they went to give a concert in Holland, which had just been liberated from the Germans. There he played the Mendelssohn violin concerto, the first performance in Europe since the Nazis had banned Mendelssohn, along with all other so called Jewish composers.

Some time later, I met his close friend and colleague, the cellist Kenneth Heath, who played saxophone in the band, and had been with him during their six years in the army. When they were together, they told stories of some of the mischievous behaviour they sometimes indulged in. Reminiscing about those times had the two of them in fits of laughter. "So," I thought, "It was not all bad."

Despite this hiatus in Raymond's career, he did have time to practise and learn an enormous repertoire - forty concertos.

"Where did you practise?" I asked

"Anywhere. Quite often in the lavatories."

It was enough to enable him to win the Carl Flesch International Violin Prize in 1946 (whilst he was still in uniform), which kick started his post-war professional life.

I was to learn about his childhood, but not until after I had met his mother and his brother Cecil. In the mean time our relationship was growing. It was easy to fall in love with him. He was very good looking, warm, funny, charming and the wonderful violin sounds emanating from his darkened room when he practised were enough to turn any young girl's head.

However, I didn't like him teasing me. I didn't understand teasing and could sometimes be upset by it. It took time for me to realise that he never meant to hurt. For example, he was very quick to pick up and point out what he considered any misuse of the English language. He was quite pedantic about it. I had never been taught any grammar, and was lost when he talked of transitive and intransitive verbs, or the misuse of "less" and "fewer" or when he got angry about incorrect punctuation. He certainly didn't think that swearing was a misuse of the language. In fact he loved being with the old Jewish musicians (who had played in bands and in the cinemas during the war) when he worked with them at recording sessions. They could swear and curse fluently in Yiddish: usually at the poor unknowing Musical Directors.

I learned to cope with the teasing, but I was very distressed that he was still seeing other women. As I have said, he was a catch and he always had an eye for a pretty girl. Usually these flirtations only lasted a short time, often only a night or two, and once or twice I plucked up the courage to ask,

"Did you have a nice time last night?"

All innocent!

"Pretty girl," came the answer, "but boring. Didn't know anything about music."

Great, I thought, that was my strong point.

And then, out of the blue, in the summer of 1951, (I was now eighteen), he asked if I would like him to teach me to drive. I was surprised and touched.

"In your precious car?" I asked.

Cars were like gold dust at that time.

"I trust you," he said. "Anyway, I will be sitting there not letting anything happen."

"Goodness, that's brave," I thought. "Maybe now I can stop worrying about the other women."

I thought about his plan, and worried about doing any damage to his treasured 1938 Standard-eight car. That would be the end of our blossoming relationship. It would be a much better idea if I had some professional lessons first, and then accepted his offer for me to practise on his car, with him as official driver. So that is what I did. The actual driving proved less difficult than I had imagined, but the car itself made problems. There were no flashing lights in those days to indicate right or left turns, only an indicator which flipped out of the relevant side of the car. The problem was that it invariably stuck and needed to be banged from the inside to make it work. In any case hand signals were imperative. You stuck your hand out of the window to turn right, round and round for left, and up and down for slowing down. The real problem was changing gears and hand signalling at the same time. I could have done with a third hand. I had six professional lessons and some practise in Raymond's car and then applied for a test.

The great day dawned. A lovely sunny morning: me in my prettiest summer dress. It's a good idea to look as pretty as possible for the male driving examiner. Something was terribly wrong with the car. The clutch was not working. Raymond tried it out.

"If you accelerate hard, and lift the clutch very slowly, it works," he said.

I tried. It did work, but would the examiner let me use this car?

When we saw him we told him the problem,

"Would you let me have a go?" I asked.

"Yes, but only if you don't blame the car if you fail."

All went well with a lot of very slow, painful changing of gears until the test which involves reversing round a corner keeping as close to the kerb as possible. I put the gear into reverse, revving as hard as I could, and the car flew backwards round the corner, into the kerb at full speed.

The bloody clutch worked perfectly in reverse.

But amazingly, I passed and have been driving ever since.

On reflection, I realised that the driving lessons were a ploy to get me into the little car, close up to him, with his hand on mine on the gearstick and the occasional kiss for when I succeeded in doing a three point turn or some other manoeuvre. I couldn't have been happier, especially as he was also taking me out and becoming very physical. He was, however, still bringing up the problem of our age difference and the fact that I was so young. It was true, but I couldn't see the problem. He certainly did not look his age (32) and he definitely never acted or thought like an older man. (This was to prove true for the rest of his life.)

Mrs. Lubel became suspicious of this growing relationship, and one night she caught me coming downstairs from my attic.

She stormed out of her bedroom, in a crumpled nightie, hair in curlers.

"And where do you think you are going?" she demanded.

I honestly had been going to have a pee in the lavatory which was next to Raymond's room. But she was on guard, wasn't going to have any shenanigans in her house.

But by the end of 1951 we were definitely a couple. Mrs. Lubel wrote to my mother to tell her what her daughter was getting up to. Little did she know that that was exactly what Gertie had been hoping for.

So now we went out together to concerts, sometimes to the pictures, for drives into the countryside or to sit amorously in the car in picturesque places such as the Serpentine Lake in Hyde Park. Once, on a romantic walk on Hampstead Heath, hand in hand, the momentary silence was broken by Raymond saying, with great excitement,

"I've just thought of an amazing fingering for that bit in the Brahms" (violin concerto).

I was hurt, he should have been thinking of me.

But I learned that the music he was working on would persist, round and round in his brain, and suddenly, out of his subconscious, an answer to a technical or musical problem would pop into his head. He continued to have sudden revelations about fingerings throughout his life. Sometimes in the middle of the night.

My daughter Gillian, who is also a violinist explained about fingering-

"Fingering" in the context of a violinist's work, could be

likened to choosing a route for a journey. There are many choices for a violinist to make when faced with a set of notes to play. This is because any note (with four exceptions) can be played on any of the 4 strings of the violin and by any one of the 4 fingers that are used. For technical ease and in order to achieve the desired musical effect, a violinist will need to choose what they consider to be the best way ("route") to play a group of notes.

Apart from what was known as heavy petting, and the fact that he was no longer going on dates with other women, I realised things were getting really serious when Raymond took me to meet his oldest friends in the London vicinity, Cedric and Joan Hirson. Cedric was a doctor, following in his father's footsteps (Doctor Hirson had been the Cohens' family doctor in Manchester) and although Cedric was a little older than Raymond, they had played cricket and other games together as children. I was quite innocent at the time of Raymond's intention of getting me vetted, just thinking that we were out for the afternoon in the semi-countryside to visit his friends. Presumably they gave him the thumbs up about me, for a little later he invited me to go up to Manchester with him to meet his mother and his brother Cecil.

Driving up to Manchester was an adventure in itself. The little car was not at all reliable and getting there without a breakdown of some sort was a triumph. On this occasion we didn't even have a puncture, and we were there in five hours. A record.

During the journey Raymond told me about his father Harry, who had been the head master of a Jewish elementary school, the Jews' School (now King David School). Both Raymond and his brother Cecil went to that school. (Each of them, on reaching eleven years old, had won a scholarship to Manchester Grammar School). Harry Cohen had an External Maths degree from London University and was a self-taught violinist.

He was Raymond's first violin teacher and had, in fact, also taught his future wife Rebecca Goldstone, his two brothers, Joe and Maurice, his eldest son Cecil and many of the young Jewish boys and girls of north Manchester. Somehow he found time and energy to conduct an amateur orchestra on Sunday mornings, and teach maths at a night school three or four evenings as week. When he did have a free day, he would take Raymond to the countryside where they would find a farm and drink milk, fresh from the cows. But he was a strict Victorian father and was not loath, when his young son had misbehaved, to take off his belt, tell his poor boy,

"Bend over and close your eyes" and belt him on his bottom.

"I always managed to get a book and stuff it in my pants first, so it didn't hurt," Raymond told me.

The family unfailingly spent two weeks of the summer holidays at Blackpool, where Harry sat on the beach, fully dressed in suit and tie, doing maths puzzles.

He died suddenly from a heart attack when he was about 62. Raymond was allowed 48 hours leave from the army, and felt the loss bitterly because he was just beginning to get to know his stern father. Any problem between them had always been about religion. Harry was strictly observant and Raymond rebelled against the rituals that, in their house, were never fun and never explained, merely imposed.

He became an ardent atheist from then on.

I took an instant dislike to Manchester as we drove through the city. It was grey, wet, and dirty.

We were passing though an even more miserable looking area when Raymond said, "This is Cheetham Hill, where we lived until I was about eight."

It was run down and dreary, with row after row of packed-together small terraced houses.

"It was a Jewish ghetto, but I was happy there," he said.

I had nothing to say. It looked awful.

"People were very poor. My father had a cupboard in the school where he kept shoes for the boys who otherwise would not have had any."

The house they moved to in Prestwich was, in comparison, very grand. It even boasted a circular tower like a fairy-tale castle and was surrounded by fields. In reality it was an Edwardian four-bedroomed house with the first indoor WC they had had. Unfortunately, the fields were soon developed into estates of small houses.

Raymond's mother, Rebecca, a beautiful woman with thick brown hair and hazel eyes, greeted me at the front door. She was quite cool towards me. Raymond, making excuses, told me later that she was shy and unsure of herself. Older brother Cecil (a conductor of an amateur orchestra), who was a taller, even more good-looking version of Raymond, was quite the opposite. I got a hug and a kiss on the cheek from him. Unfortunately he couldn't stay long that evening, and dinner was a stiff and awkward affair. Raymond had always been his mother's blue-eyed boy, and although she wanted him to be married and happy, I felt sure she wasn't very pleased with this young girl.

"So, you are from South Africa?" she said. "How do you like England?"

"I'm very happy here, it is all new to me and so exciting."

"You must find us all very poor coming from such a rich family."

What! Where did she get that from?

"All those lovely clothes," she continued.

"Actually my mother made all my clothes until very recently, and we certainly aren't rich. My father only has a small shop, no other money."

That shut her up for the moment.

Her big disappointment in her lovely son was his strong anti-religious attitude. So the conversation between them had a lot to do with that, but I think she appreciated the time and attention he gave her since the death of her husband. She was not sociable, did not have a lot of friends, and had problems getting on with Cecil. Raymond loved her and felt sorry for her loneliness.

We stayed in Manchester for a few days during which time I got to know a little more about the family, and some stories of Raymond's childhood.

Raymond and me in 1952

In the Army 19yrs old

7 years later

Raymond's parents - Harry and Rebecca

Cecil's Story

Cecil

As Raymond always said, "I was born a violinist, lived a violinist and will die a violinist." I think some words about that sentence are appropriate here.

Well, he wasn't actually born with a violin under his chin, but at two years old, his mother told me, she had stood him on the dining room table with a violin and bow. He was already holding both correctly. Then she moved one of his fingers up and down on a string, and between the two of them, they produced a version of the "Sheik of Araby".

A picture of him at three, shows him smiling and holding the violin and the bow in exactly the same way as he would do for the rest of his life.

And so it continued. His father gave him his first lesson, and then passed him on to his brother Maurice. Maurice played the violin at the cinemas and the lessons lasted a year or two until Lionel Falkman arrived in Manchester. Falkman had studied with the legendary teacher Leopold Auer (the teacher of all

202

the great Russian violinists) and now he led an orchestra at the Paramount Theatre (Cinema). Later, and for many years, he led the "Apache" band at Lyons Corner House in Tottenham Court Road, London. Raymond had his lessons in the dressing room, whilst Lionel changed out of his Gypsy costume into a suit.

And then Henry Holst, the Danish violinist, arrived from Berlin in 1931/32. Before leaving Germany when the Nazis began to take power, he had been the leader of the Berlin Philharmonic Orchestra and was now Professor at the Northern College of Music. Holst became Raymond's teacher from then on.

Aged fifteen, Raymond really wanted to leave school and continue studying with Mr. Holst at the College. His father was not at all keen on this, and would only agree to it if he proved his talent and ability by winning the Brodsky Scholarship (the most prestigious entrance award). Raymond won the scholarship having played the Goldmark concerto, but Mr. Cohen was still not sure that this was the route he wanted his son to take, so he went to see the principal of the college to ask if he thought Raymond was soloist material or would he be spending his life somewhere in an orchestra. The Halle Orchestra (Manchester's orchestra) only performed once a week and only in the winter months and Mr. Cohen knew that this would not generate a decent living, beside which, it would not in any way be life-enhancing. So he was happy when Robert Forbes (the Principal), assured him of Raymond's outstanding talent. Although he was at least three years younger than most of his fellow students at college, he soon became the star pupil, playing at all the concerts, giving BBC broadcasts and concerts all over the north of England and getting rave reviews from the newspapers.

He had lived all his life, up until then, in a solely masculine (except for his mother) milieu and was shy and diffident with girls. There were some gorgeous girls (especially in the drama department), whom he fancied madly, but being so much younger, and for the first year or so, so much smaller, it made his quest virtually impossible. The best he was able to do was to walk the chosen girl to the bus stop.

Aged fifteen or sixteen, he became the youngest ever player in the Halle orchestra. Sitting at the back of the violins, during the first rehearsal and concert, he was terrified when he discovered that he didn't properly understand "counting." As a soloist he could rely on his ear and his knowledge of the sound of the music so this problem had not arisen. The answer was to go back to his father, the mathematician, who very quickly sorted it out.

During the time he was in the orchestra, the list of soloists was legendary. Sergei Rachmaninoff played his own second piano concerto, and Raymond remembered hardly being able to play, while listening awestruck to his idols: the violinists Fritz Kreisler and Jasha Heifetz. Amongst the conductors, Thomas Beecham was both inspiring and terrifying. He once stopped the orchestra with a loud roar in the middle of a live broadcast concert because the horns had "cracked" on a number of notes. (It was quite common in those days. Nowdays, since improvements to the instrument, it almost never happens). Much to the their embarrassment, the orchestra had to begin the movement all over again.

At seventeen, and in the following summer season, he led the hugely popular Blackpool South Pier Orchestra on the pier itself in their twice-daily concerts of popular and light classical music, which often included a violin solo. There were also comedy evenings (he loved making people laugh) and as he also had a girlfriend there, these months were, in some ways, the most enjoyable of his life.

But it all came crashing down with the outbreak of war. He managed to postpone his entry into the army to give himself another year of study and, thinking that this would be the last performance of his life, he gave a remarkable concert with the Halle orchestra, playing three concertos in one evening: Bach, Mendelssohn and Brahms.

But I wanted to know something about his life when he wasn't playing the fiddle, the part he always said he didn't remember, so I asked his brother Cecil to tell me about it.

Cecil was nearly five years older than his only sibling. He also had learned the violin with his father and it must have been very hard for him, aged seven or eight, to suddenly find his young brother, the little genius, getting all the attention.

But as the years went by, Cecil became Raymond's mentor. He took the place of their father, Harry, taking him to concerts, and later acting as his unofficial agent.

So here is Cecil's story, his memories of their childhood together, given to me with many ums and ahs and a great deal of raucous laughter:

He was my baby brother and we shared a room and a bed and were, in many ways, very close, but because he was so much younger, I was always the dominant person in our play together.

There was a game we played called "under and over the bed". It was a sort of pillow fight. I always managed to be on top of the bed whacking Raymond who was under it. I made up stories about the buses that went from near our house into town and back. I transformed them into various members of our family and told my gullible brother of the races they took part in whilst we were asleep.

We invented a brother called Freddy. Freddy, unfortunately, only lived for sixty seconds, dying by banging his head on his bed post, but during his lifetime could do amazing maths puzzles, play four or five different instruments, score a century at cricket, in fact Freddy could do anything our imaginations could conjure up.

We played cricket in the fields before they were built over, and later in the garden. I was in charge and gave the instructions Raymond was meant to obey. Our friend Cedric, who often played with us, amazed us once by announcing, "Cecil, let him use his own discretion". (What a vocabulary for a 10-year old?) It became a family catchword.

We played a lot of Monopoly. I had a habit, late at night, of saying, "Just another quick game." Of course there is no such thing as a quick game of monopoly.

And then I started taking girls out for walks and Raymond would follow us around. He became known as "trailer".

Sometimes we gave concerts together. I would accompany him on the piano. I was a very bad pianist, couldn't accurately play the part, but could always find the right chord, so that was OK. We played little solos in the cinemas and at barmitzvahs and weddings.

Every year we spent a two-week holiday in Blackpool. We both loved it. There were three piers and each one would have different bands. The South Pier, where Raymond later played, was always more select, but there were jazz bands and gypsy bands on the other piers and we could sit on deck chairs and listen to them; it was all free. We also spent a lot of time in the Pleasure Beach or Amusement Park, not going for rides, but playing games such as rolling pennies, throwing balls at the coconut shy, or laughing hysterically at our distorted reflections in the Hall of Mirrors. At home, Raymond went to the cinema twice a week with our parents: Wednesdays and Saturday. He loved the films and was thrilled by the music. Very romantic with swooping violins. This was an inspiration. He definitely wanted to play for the movies.

Most importantly, we spent an enormous amount of time listening to music, at first on the crystal radio set we made ourselves and then on wirelesses, which had improved so much, that we could listen to performances from places with strange names such as Hilversum, and from as far afield as Moscow.

There was an amazing series of recitals given by international celebrity musicians. We went to all of these and Raymond would be spellbound by violinists such as Misha Elman, Fritz Kreisler, Szigeti or Heifetz and would go home after the concert and try to imitate the sound and style of each of them. He would spend the night playing, walking up and down in our music room in the dark, determined to achieve that. His teacher, Mr. Holst, once told him to stop trying to play Mozart the way Heifetz did, and to find his own voice which, of course, he eventually did.

So we were back to music, but I was delighted and relieved to know that this man, with whom I had fallen in love, had not been treated like a child prodigy and forced to practise in order to achieve fame. It was as normal a childhood as it was possible to have for anyone with such a remarkable talent.

Raymond at 3 years old

Henry Holst

South Pier Orchestra Blackpool

Fifth Movement

Appassionato

Life and Love

If Music be the Food of Love - Coloured Drypoint

Amore

Back in London I became aware that letters had been coming from my mother over the past few months telling me that the family were planning to come to London to live here for a while. I had not taken it in. I was having too good a time and I was in love but, in the spring of 1952, I realised with a shock, that in July, it was going to happen. My parents asked if I could find them appropriate accommodation: somewhere for us all to be together, and with space for a piano so that Lorraine and I could both practise. Of course I had very mixed feelings. It would be good to have all the family back together again, to live somewhere I could call my own, and to leave the tension of the Lubel house, but I would be moving away from Raymond. I had no idea how that would work out. I didn't have the courage to discuss this with him, so I would just have to wait and see.

We set out together to find somewhere for the four Israels. Neither of us had any idea about property, but we managed to find a wonderful flat in Wedderburn Road, Hampstead. £10 a week was more than they had wanted to pay, but it had three bedrooms and a very large sitting room and I was sure they were going to like it.

So one morning in July, there I was at the docks in Southampton when mother, father and sister arrived with multitudes of packing cases and their car - a great big American Chevy. A very rare beast in England. Wow!

I had no real idea of why they had made the enormous decision to sell up their home and their business and emigrate. Maybe they presumed (correctly) that I would not be going back to South Africa in the near future and they wanted the family to be together. Maybe my mother wanted Lorraine to have lessons from my teacher, Illona Kabos, or maybe they could see what the future held back home with the beginning of unrest and resistance against Apartheid. Whatever the reason, we all moved into the flat in Hampstead.

My mother was delighted to see that I had lost weight and

also grown a bit, but Issie took the opposite view. He thought I looked as if I needed a holiday, after all I had worked so hard and had not had a break, so he took me to the sea-side, to Perranporth in Cornwall for a week, where we sat on the beach and learned never to try to swim in the English sea. It was freezing. I thought I would become paralysed and drown. Mostly I waited impatiently for letters from Raymond. I was still really not sure of his intentions and needed reassurance. The post in those days was amazing. Any letter posted before six in the evening would be delivered anywhere in Britain by the next day, and to my joy and relief a letter arrived almost every day.

Before moving into Wedderburn Road, I had to pack up my things, and say goodbye to everyone at no.31. I was really fearful that not being in daily contact with Raymond would weaken, or even end our relationship, but that didn't happen. He would come over whenever he had a free moment, have tea or a meal that my mother would make (something new for her), and best of all, we often played violin and piano pieces together. There was even a suggestion that we would do a concert together in the spring. He got on very well with my Mum and Dad and treated Lorraine like a naughty little sister. She had started piano lessons with Miss Kabos and was taking classes in other subjects, including French. Raymond teased her so much about her terrible accent that she gave up French altogether.

I was worried that winter in London might threaten Gertie's health. There was the possibility that her asthma would worsen in the cold and the polluted atmosphere, but she seemed to survive it well, even when, in December 1952, the "Great Smog" occurred. Something about the weather conditions and the pollution caused by coal-burning fires, caused the worst foggy conditions that London had ever experienced. During London's regular "Pea-soupers" people were wont to say: "Its so foggy I can't see my hand in front of my face," which was an exaggeration but, for four days in December of that year, it was actually true. About twelve thousand people died and because of it, in 1956, the government brought in the Clean Air Act, eliminating the burning of coal in private homes and in factories. My memory of it is walking in front of Raymond's car with a torch so that he could find the pavement and park it. He couldn't drive home, so we pulled out cushions from the sofa and he spent the nights on the floor of the sitting room. (Well, at least part of the nights).

Living so near Hampstead Heath meant that we often went there for walks. It's a huge area so there was always somewhere new to explore. It was on one of these walks, on a rare sunny day, when, at last, he plucked up courage and asked me to marry him. I did not refuse.

My parents were delighted with our news, I don't think Raymond went so far as to ask my father for my hand in marriage, which was still the convention in those days, but Issie felt very strongly that I must have a diamond engagement ring. I didn't really want one. I would much rather have had a coloured stone in an antique setting, but Issie had such a strong belief in the value of diamonds, that we took his advise and found a pretty ring which pleased us all.

My mother declared that she didn't believe in long engagements and in this case I agreed with her, the sooner we were together the better. But I didn't realise until later, how stressful arranging a wedding and finding a home at the same time, would be.

First we had to find a date when Raymond would definitely not have a concert. It was difficult. Eventually March 8th was decided upon and Gertie set about organising a fairy-tale wedding; the climax of our fairy-tale love story; our magical meeting; falling in love and finally marrying. I thought that it was miraculous that from 6000 miles away I had landed in a very ordinary terrace house, in a very ordinary North London suburb and that Raymond was already settled in the same ordinary house, having moved, after leaving Manchester, from one form of lodging to another, finally settling for the ordinary house in Muswell Hill.

It not only had to be a fairy-tale wedding it also had to be a Jewish wedding. In those days it was always the bride's family who hosted the wedding, but I had no idea how they were going to do this. They had only been in London for about six months and knew very few people, but nothing deterred them. They discovered that Gunter's Tea Room in Curzon Street would be available to stage the whole thing: the wedding ceremony and the reception; an afternoon wedding, and a tea-dance. Gunter's was a rather posh tea place, famous for its wedding cakes, having made Queen Victoria's. We too had a wedding cake, ours with a piano and violin on top.

In fact we had the whole caboodle. Me, in a meringue wedding dress, and all the men in morning suits and top hats. How they managed to persuade Raymond into that I cannot imagine. He hated that sort of thing. He really must have loved me. Monte Lubel, in his officer's uniform, was the best man, and my sister Lorraine, in yellow tulle, was the bridesmaid. We had a band and dancing and about 100 guests.

There were family and old friends from Manchester; the residents of number 31; some of Raymond's colleague and friends, and some of mine. It adds up. We didn't belong to a synagogue, but having registered the marriage at Hampstead Town Hall, the formal Jewish ceremony took place at Gunter's. Raymond may have been dressed for the part, but as we stood solemnly under the chuppa (the wedding canopy) with the rabbi proceeding slowly with the ceremony and singing loudly with a huge vibrato, he could no longer control the laughter that, although his shoulders had been shaking, he had until then kept in check. It burst out of him with a loud guffaw and he continued to giggle uncontrollably. It infected the whole congregation and everyone was convulsed with laughter, including the organist, a friend, who then forgot to play for us to walk out at the end. It was all good fun, after which we left for our three-day honeymoon in Bournemouth.

At Southampton Dock

Issie unpacking at Wedderburn Road

Cutting the cake

Left to right: Raymond, me, Gertie, Issie,
Rebecca (Raymond's mother) Lorraine, Monte Lubel

Santa Margarita

After our wedding, we spent a three-day honeymoon at a hotel in Bournemouth. It was only three days because immediately after our return to London, Raymond would be giving the first performance in England of the Ernest Bloch violin concerto and needed many hours of practising time for that. So, although enjoying what I had expected to be doing on honeymoon, the rest of my time was spent sitting in a chair listening to the Bloch concerto. So we decided that we definitely needed, or anyway wanted, a proper honeymoon, and as Raymond had two free weeks in June, our plan was to drive to the Italian Riviera - without the violin.

In preparation for this adventure, I had a page in my South African passport stamped to prove that I was now a legitimately married woman, my father spent many happy hours restoring our 1938 Standard 8 car, and we had each withdrawn from the bank the full £25 we were allowed to take out of the country at that time.

Someone had told Raymond of a wonderful resort on the Mediterranean called Santa Margarita and with that as our aim, we set off for Dover and the cross-channel ferry. We passed through the customs, drove the car onto the ship and were enjoying the smooth crossing when there was an announcement on the tannoy.

"Would anyone who is not a French citizen please come to the Purser's office where an official will stamp your passports so that you can land quickly at Calais."

"You stay here, darling," my newly-wed husband said, "I'll take your passport".

He was not gone long.

"Darling, Do you have a visa?"

"What? What's a visa?"

I thought of rummaging though my bag to see if such as thing existed but decided I needed to visit the customs official to find out what he was talking about.

Well, it seemed that as I had a South African passport I wouldn't be allowed to land in France without a stamp in it from a French consulate. Why hadn't any one told me about this before? I had seen the Consul at South Africa House, passed though customs at Dover, but not a word had ever been said.

Our dismayed and forlorn faces must have touched the Purser.

"Wait here," he told us, "I'll talk to the Captain".

Time passed whilst the coast of France grew relentlessly nearer and nearer.

But here was the Captain. "Well," he said, "this is your lucky day". (Who was he kidding?)

"This ship is making a return trip because earlier today bad weather forced us to cancel the first sailing. So this is my plan. Mr. Cohen will drive the car off the ship at Calais, park it at the harbour, and then re-board. You, young lady will stay here. I have discovered that there is a French Consulate officer in Folkstone who is working this Saturday afternoon and I've been in touch with him. He will give you the necessary visa. I have also laid on a car and a driver who will drive you there, wait for you, and bring you back in time for the return trip to Calais. But it will be tight, so be as quick as you can."

We were speechless. What an amazing man!

When we arrived in Calais, Raymond drove the car off the ship and parked it. I hung over the rails wishing that I was with him and that we were happily driving off into unknown territory. I had to remind myself that if we were lucky, we would be doing that later that day. And soon he was back with me on the deck and we were once again at sea, the white cliffs of Dover slowly getting nearer.

As soon as the ship docked, the gangplank was lowered and we hurtled down and into a waiting car. Arriving In Folkstone, the driver seemed to know where to find the Consulate Office, which was hidden in a narrow street above a run-down shop. We rushed upstairs and knocked on the door.

"Entrée, entrée".

We opened the door to see a tall, wiry, elderly man with

wispy grey hair and glasses perched on the end of his nose.

He jabbered away in fast French that we didn't understand but indicated a woman who was sitting at the desk. He obviously had to deal with her before he could see us. Oh dear.

We jittered about just outside the door, opening it occasionally to remind him we were there and, after what seemed an eternity, the woman left.

Without waiting for an invitation we barged in and handed him my passport.

"Ah, oui. Asseyez-vous, asseyez-vous".

We sat whilst he rummaged in a drawer and came up with a large stamping device, which he inked up on a pad. Then he thumbed though my passport, found an empty page and banged the stamp down.

"Merci beaucoup", we chorused trying to grab the passport from him.

"Non, non, non." He took the passport out of our hands and very, very, slowly began to explain in hesitant English what the visa was for. He shook his head. It seemed he wasn't happy with the quality of the printing, so pulling a pen out of his pocket, he proceeded to write in large spidery letters all over the printed page whilst expounding on each word.

Raymond now entirely lost his cool.

"Can I use your phone?" Without waiting for an answer he marched up to a telephone hanging on the wall. I had not realised until that moment that the Captain had given him the ship's number and had asked us to ring and tell him what was happening, and when we would be back.

"Hello," Raymond virtually shouted, "I am so relieved to hear your voice. We are delayed here."

And then, after a pause,

"OK. Thanks." He replaced the receiver.

"What did he say?"

"He says they are still at the docks but we must hurry".

The Consul now woke up to the urgency of the situation and handed over the passport. I grabbed it and we raced down the stairs to the waiting car.

Our chauffeur must have dreamed of being a racing driver. As the crow flies, Folkstone is only six miles from Dover, but the road was very hilly with sharp bends and curves.

His car only had a top speed of about fifty or sixty miles an hour and the suspension left a lot to be desired, but he put his foot down hard and we rocked and swung from side to side until we reached the customs shed. "Good Luck," he shouted as we slammed out of the car. Holding hands we ran, our footsteps echoing thunderously in the huge, now absolutely empty corrugated tin shed. It felt and sounded more and more like something out of a film but now we were onto the docks. And there was the ship looming above us, the Captain and Purser hanging over the railing watching and waiting.

"Up you come, we have kept the ship waiting for you," they shouted as we clambered up the steps.

The gangplank was raised and almost immediately the ferry moved off.

"Well, I'm glad you made it," the Captain said. "Go and have a drink and relax. All will be well."

It took a while for us to stop shaking but the captain was right. The sea was smooth and the customs officer on board smiled at us as we handed in our passports.

Just as we were about to leave the ship at Calais our guardian angel reappeared.

"Can we pay you for the extra journey?" we asked.

"No, it is my wedding present to you. Have a long and happy life. And don't forget to drive on the right."

That was the beginning of the journey which would eventually land us on the Italian coast. Along the way we had to find consulate offices to get visas for me before we could enter Switzerland or Italy. They were filled with refugees, (there were still so many displaced people from the war) who were sitting sadly but patiently with battered suitcases and tattered children waiting and hoping to be allowed to go somewhere, anywhere.

Our very old car behaved as well as it was possible but had

to be filled with water, have its plugs cleaned and its punctured tyres changed at regular intervals. It chuffed its way up the St Bernard Pass with many stops for a rest and reached the summit in a spectacular thunderstorm. This was the border between Switzerland and Italy and the guard there invited us into his hut to wait for the storm to clear.

There, packed into a small room, were the dozen or so British bikers who had waved and cheered as they passed us on their way up. I was quite intimidated at being in such a small space with these huge, scary looking men, but I was wrong. Their banter, wit and jollity turned the hour or two spent waiting for the storm to pass into a party. I was sorry to wave them goodbye as they roared off down the mountain.

We followed them down, and in our ignorance expected the sea to be appearing soon. Instead we were driving through the seemingly endless Maritime Alps, up and down hill after hill, round and round more bends, so it was a great relief when we eventually hit the coast.

"Now we only have to drive along this road until we arrive at Santa Margarita," was the thought.

But we were tired and hungry. It was now nine o'clock, and driving though the village of Laigueglia, we spied a hotel and decided to leave Santa Margarita for another day. The owner showed us a room. We had lost our English diffidence on our journey and now asked to see rooms before agreeing to take them. No one seemed to mind, and we had also learned to say no when the room looked even more dirty and flea-ridden than was tolerable.

This room was wonderful. Large and light with windows on three sides and a big clean bed. The front window looked directly out over the sea, the beach being on each side of the hotel. Perfect. A dream room.

"What can we get you to eat?" we were asked. At ten o'clock at night?

"We can offer you steak and salad and mountain strawberries with cream. Would that be OK?"

Would it!

This was the best meal we had eaten for years. France was still so battered and poor as a result of the war that the food had not lived up to our expectations. Steak and cream were unobtainable in England where we were still fiercely rationed. And tiny mountain strawberries? A bliss completely unheard of.

We were definitely not going to Santa Margarita. We had found heaven and there we stayed until it was time to head for home.

On the beach at Laiguelia

Now we felt like seasoned travellers. We bought a proper map, decided on a quicker route and headed off for Calais. All went well, except as we travelled further and further north, the little car began to show its age. We willed it along and hoped that with care and attention it would make it back in one piece. Three quarters of the journey had been completed when things got decidedly worse. Strange noises emanated from the engine and the car began to judder.

"We have to find a garage. It's going to blow up and kill us," I shouted.

Raymond could only think that he had soon to be back in England for some concerts. Dates in the diary were sacrosanct.

"No, no. I've got to get back even if we have to push the fucking thing," he raved.

We had just reached Chateau Thierry, a little town in the north of France when there was a loud bang and the car came to a shuddering halt. Now we definitely had to find a garage and find out what was happening. Fortunately there was one near at hand. The mechanic took one look at the car and threw up his arms.

"Kaput! Kaput! Finished". It was the big-end, what ever that was, and it was irreparable.

One of the things we had remembered to do before we left London was to pay for a five star insurance for the car from the AA and now was the time to use it. We found a phone and rang them, told them the story, and asked what our next move should be. The answer was to have the car towed to the railway station, give the AA all the details and leave them to deal with getting the poor broken thing back to us. The garage agreed to transport the car, but now we were stranded with very little money and no plan B. The only thing we could think of doing was to get a train from Chateau Thierry to Paris, spend the night there, get another train to Calais, and then somehow get home.

But there were hours to spend before the train was due. How to fill the time. We wandered about for a bit with our suitcases but there was nothing in this place. And then we saw a cinema. In England cinemas showed films on a loop and you could go in anytime, see some of the film, watch the B movie and the news and then watch the film up to the moment when you had first arrived. Or stay and see it all again. All for the same price.

We expected to find the same thing here. Watching a film, even in French, would pass the time. We bought tickets and went in to find the place brightly lit and completely empty. We sat and waited, and waited. Something would happen any moment wouldn't it? But nothing did and finally we went to find out what was going on.

"The film will not start until 7pm," they said. Why on earth had they sold us tickets and let us in? What did they imagine we were going to do in there for two or three hours? So we walked slowly to the station and sat in the waiting room until the train arrived.

The area around Paris Nord, where the train stopped, was sleazy and run down. Loose plaster and black water stains disfigured the walls. Prostitutes lined the streets. There were lots of hotels, most of them brothels, but we found a room, not even asking to see it first. It was all we could afford. The next morning we used our very last francs for the train to Calais.

Now we were on the docks. We had no money at all but somehow we had to get on board and across to England. We were chatting to a young couple with a car, who were going back to London.

"I know this is a terrible cheek," Raymond said, "but could we hitch a ride with you? The ferry costs are the same for two or four passengers so that would not really be cheating".

"Why not? Hop in".

What a relief, we were heading home. At Dover, just as we about to join our new friends in their car and drive off the ferry, Raymond noticed a nail in one of the tyres. Hoping to do a good turn, he removed the nail. There was a loud hissing sound and the tyre subsided. I won't repeat the words uttered by our hosts, but changing the tyre involved emptying the boot, which was loaded with suitcases (including ours) to find the spare wheel, jacking up the car and holding up dozens of people waiting to land.

Although not a word was spoken on the journey back to London, they dropped us at Hyde Park Corner and went on their way. It seemed ridiculous, but we didn't even have the money for a phone call, so having found a phone box, I reversed the charges and feeling like a small child, I called my father.

"Daddy, can you come and pick us up?" And he did.

Home: Holders Hill Road

On our return we moved into the house we were buying with the help of a deposit from my Dad. It was a three-bedroomed semi in Hendon. It fitted our specific requirements: a place where our music would not disturb the neighbours. It had two sitting rooms, one for the piano and a separate one for violin practice. Soon after we settled in, our adjacent neighbour rang our door-bell.

"I have heard the music," she said.

"Oh dear," I said. "Is it disturbing you?"

"No, no. My husband used to be a musician. He played in nightclubs, but he was always out all night, not getting home until three or four in the morning. I hated it, and so he decided to do something else."

"What does he do now?"

"He's a butcher".

What she neglected to say was that now he left home at about 2.30 in the morning to go to the market! We would hear his car pulling out of the garage. I hope she thought that that was better.

And then there was Julian. One morning there was a knock at our front door. I opened it and found, to my surprised, a tiny figure in bathing trunks and bare feet. Julian aged 4.

"Hello," I said.

"What are you doing here?" (Julian was the son of our neighbours, two doors down.)

"How's your central heating?" he asked.

"We don't have any central heating. Have you?"

"Of course," he said and turned to go.

I took him home. His mother was relieved to see him.

"He keeps running away," she said.

"We caught him at the bus stop with his bucket and spade the other day: about to leave home."

We became good friends, even though I envied her central heating.

As I told Julian, we didn't have central heating in our house, but we had one radiator in the hall, fed by a coke-burning boiler in the kitchen. It was supposed to take the chill off the house, but it barely did that. However, I managed to keep the sitting room warm (the room with the piano) with a raging fire, even though coal was still rationed. We would use small, fallen, branches of wood that we collected on our walks in parks or on the Heath. That seemed to do the trick. Pouncing on suitable pieces of wood became a game we continued to play for years, long after the wood was no longer needed for warmth.

1927 Monito Top Fridge

We had no furniture for the house except a bed and some deck chairs, but the Datnow cousins had promised us a "G-plan" armchair as a wedding present when it became available. The kitchen however, was equipped, not only with a table and two chairs, but a fridge, a 1927 "Monito Top" which we bought from the previous owners of the house. It was a treasure. We became part of the elite group of 2% of the population of Great Britain, who had a fridge. We were told that on no condition should we move it because any movement would cause the gas in the tubes at the top to break. After a couple of years it was in the way, so we took a chance and moved it into the larder. It continued to work. Six years later we moved it into our new house, and it continued to work. It was still working when we renovated the kitchen six years after that. But then it had to go.

I knew nothing at all about housekeeping, I had never done a stroke of housework, never dusted or swept anything, never made a bed, never even made a cup of tea and certainly had never done any laundry. Not even washed my knickers. But I did know about reading, and as soon as I had a recipe book to read and follow, I became quite a proficient cook. I realised that if you could read, you could cook. There were no books on housekeeping so I'm afraid I did not become proficient at that. Eventually I had a cleaner (known then as a charlady) who kept the mess down to an acceptable level.

The other thing that was new since my marriage was, of course, my name. In those days a woman automatically took on the name of her husband. I was now Mrs *Raymond* Cohen and everyone, except friends and family, always called me Mrs Cohen, never Anthya. I was nineteen and for some time I was unsure who was being addressed, it was surely someone much older and more grown up than me. So when the problem of choosing a name for our newly formed musical partnership arose, I was determined to retain something of my birthright – my unmarried name. One week before our wedding we had played (in Belfast) our first concert as a Duo. It went so well, that we decided that we would go on playing together forever. As a "Duo" each partner has an equal part to play in the performance. I was therefore, not just an accompanist ("At the piano" was an expression used inaccurately), and so a decision had to be made on the name of the Duo.

Cecil, who was still very involved in Raymond's career, said that the Cohen Israel Duo sounded more like a firm of Jewish tailors than a chamber music team.

Raymond couldn't change his name, he was already too well known. I felt that playing as Anthya Cohen somehow reduced my identity, so I cut out the "I S" from ISRAEL (my maiden name) and we became the Cohen Rael Duo. I have played professionally as Anthya Rael ever since.

The Cohen Ruel Duo.

Coda

So here I am 16 years after the initial attempts I described in "Prelude," still sitting at the piano which remains a beast demanding my time and energy to achieve the music I can hear in my head - the impossible, perfect rendition - but at this time, learning a whole new repertoire and spending many hours, sharing the music with the man I love.

Looking back over those 16 years I would like to quote William Boyd, who said

"...all life amounts to in the end is the aggregate of the good luck and the bad luck you have experienced..."

I was blessed with an enormous amount of good luck. Starting with the good fortune to have been born with a talent and the advantage of having parents who did everything in their power to enable that talent to flourish.

The luck to have had amazing teachers and to cap it all, the extraordinary luck to find myself in Muswell Hill where I would, by an even more extraordinary piece of good luck, meet Raymond and marry him. It was in many ways a match made in heaven which not only lasted for 58 years but initially enabled me to jump instantly into the world of professional music-making, by becoming Raymond's pianist/partner.

Raymond wrote, on our 50th wedding anniversary:

"The Cohen Rael Duo has been a central part of our lives, and playing together is, for us, as natural as breathing. We argue over details, but we are always as one about the broad concept of music. I suppose that applies just as much to our marriage."

How lucky was that!

It is said that one makes one's own luck, but it is impossible unless there is the initial spark which can be fanned into life, and I had that in buckets.

There were times in the following years when I would superstitiously question all this good fortune, it surely could not carry on, and inevitably, life brought its downturns, which were at times almost unbearable, but the good luck fate had decreed for me always, in the long run, won the day.

230